THE FISH'S EYE

THE FISH'S EYE

ESSAYS ABOUT ANGLING

AND THE OUTDOORS

IAN FRAZIER

FARRAR, STRAUS AND GIROUX

NEW YORK

Farrar, Straus and Giroux
19 Union Square West, New York 10003

Copyright © 2002 by Ian Frazier
Distributed in Canada by Douglas & McIntyre Ltd.
Printed in the United States of America
First edition, 2002

Grateful acknowledgment is made to *Audubon*, *The New Yorker*, *Outside*,
and *Sports Afield*, where these pieces first appeared.

Library of Congress Cataloging-in-Publication Data
Frazier, Ian.
    The fish's eye / Ian Frazier.— 1st ed.
        p.   cm.
    ISBN 0–374–15520–8 (hardcover : alk. paper)
    1. Fishing.   I. Title.

SH441 .F754 2002
799.1—dc21

                                                                    2001054451

Designed by Jonathan D. Lippincott

www.fsgbooks.com

1   3   5   7   9   10   8   6   4   2

TO DON ERSKINE

CONTENTS

THE FISH'S EYE

ANGLERS

On the paved shores of the Harlem Meer (one of six ponds in the city's park system which the State Department of Environmental Conservation—in cooperation with the New York City Parks Department, the New York City Department of the Aging, and the New York State Sea Grant—stocked with bullhead catfish on June 27 as part of an urban fishing program designed to stimulate city dwellers' interest in fishing and the outdoors), on a weekday afternoon in July:

"Gregory, how much worm should I use?"

"What you got there is enough, Andrew. Bet with your head, not over it."

Across the pond, a man standing under the trees started playing a three-note progression on the trumpet over and over again, holding each note a long time.

A boy pulled up a white tube sock with a yellow stripe and a blue stripe which had been dangling in the water, and something scuttled off it.

"Look, Gregory! Look at the lobster!"

"That ain't no lobster, fool, that's a crayfish. Throw him back. Throw him back to his mama."

An empty can of Sunkist orange (the new soft drink introduced a couple of months ago) came drifting by.

"Did you pass this year?"

"Yeah, man, 'course I passed."

Across the pond, the man with the trumpet started playing each note in the three-note progression four times and in such a way as to hit it differently each time.

A plastic terrestrial globe came floating by, with just Antarctica above the waterline.

"We had a nice fish, but some people took it."

The arm of a Negro doll came floating by.

"Oh, man, my line's stuck. I have got to get it off. I have *got* to get it off."

"Pull on it, Derek."

"I don't get my line off, I can't get back in my house. I got my keys on there for a sinker."

The line came free, revealing a set of keys on an "I ♥ NY" key ring from a savings bank.

The man with the trumpet started playing "I Get a Kick Out of You."

An empty bag of Wise onion-garlic potato chips came floating by.

Two girls with their hair in cornrows took a look at four catfish in a yellow plastic bucket. "These boys should let the fish go," one girl said.

"Are you kidding? Those fish could die out in that water," the other girl said.

(1978)

HARLEM AND HUDSON

A_t the Seventy-ninth Street Boat Basin in New York City, on Labor Day, about fifty people are fishing in the Hudson River. There is no shore, no beach—there is a walkway paved with asphalt, a railing, and a concrete drop into the dark-olive water.

A little boy sitting on a plastic tricycle in the tunnel leading to the Boat Basin—the tunnel under the West Side Highway— sees a motorboat go by in the part of the river framed by the tunnel mouth. "Look at that fas'-movin' object!" he says.

One of the fishermen starts to reel in quickly. His rod is bent. When he pulls his line over the railing, it looks as if he has a giant hook on the end of his line. It is an eel that has kind of seized in that position for a moment. The eel starts to wiggle and flop so wildly that its body describes a blurry sphere. The fisherman yells in Spanish, and then slaps the eel down on the pavement with a full overhead motion of his fishing rod. He starts to kick the still-squirming eel along the pavement. He kicks it quite a distance.

A man who lives off the very rich garbage containers outside the fenced-off dock for the biggest yachts decides to throw away his belongings, which he carries in two black Hefty bags. He throws the bags into the river, but they don't float very far away. Then he holds up his hand to stop some people who are walking by, and taking a lightbulb from an inner coat pocket, he also throws that into the river, much farther than the bags. He looks at the people, winks, and puts his finger to his lips.

Another of the fishermen finishes a Kool cigarette and tosses it into a yellow bucket at his feet. In the bucket, along with a few other Kool butts turning brown in auras of brown stain, are two striped bass, both over twenty inches.

Farther upriver, but still within New York City limits, a hundred and fifty or two hundred people are fishing along the shore from Spuyten Duyvil, where the Harlem River empties into the Hudson, up to the Refined Sugars and Syrups Company plant, at the boundary of Riverdale. Along this section of river there are neighborhoods of fishermen: from the point where the Harlem and the Hudson meet to about a quarter mile upstream are black fishermen and fisherwomen and their families; beyond that, farther upstream, the fishermen and fisherwomen are mostly Spanish-speaking; and beyond that, they are mostly Japanese. The Harlem River for the few hundred yards downstream from the Spuyten Duyvil railroad station to the Hudson is a mixed neighborhood, with some whites, some Puerto Ricans, and some blacks. Amtrak passenger and freight trains, to and from New York, and Conrail commuter trains run on tracks within forty feet of the water's edge. Along the tracks are third rails with the warning "Danger 700 Volts" on them. Between the tracks are white pieces of paper with the heading "Message to Our Commuters" blowing around, and a copy of *Tennis USA* magazine with Björn Borg on the cover and ads about how to work your way through college by playing tennis on the inside.

Big rocks put there by the railroad are along the shore. In the Spanish-speaking section of riverfront, two men and a woman are sitting on the rocks. One of the men has no shirt on, and the other man is wearing a gray shirt with flowers so pink that they attract bees. Bees are actually buzzing around him, but he does not notice. The woman is reading an article in a magazine. The title of the article is *"Billy Martin en la Despedida: 'Soy un Yankee Ahora y Siempre.'* " The two men are fishing with eight-foot surf-casting rods, using sandworms for bait. One of the men snags a sandworm out of the bait carton with a plastic comb, and then he uses the comb to cut the sandworm in half on the rock. There are flashes of white in the river some distance out, and the other man jumps up and shouts, *"Una mancha! Una mancha!"* The man who was baiting up quickly casts to where the other man pointed. The English translation of *una mancha* is "a spot or a stain," but it can also mean a birthmark, a rash, or any kind of surface disturbance. People shout it along this section of river when they see striped bass chasing baitfish.

A Puerto Rican family crosses the railroad tracks: a man, his wife, his brother, his sister-in-law, her nephew, and two babies in strollers. The men are carrying rods, bait, tackle boxes, folding chairs, a cooler, and a plastic bucket with ice and eight-ounce party bottles of Miller beer. The women are pushing the strollers, lifting each carefully over the live rail. The older man is the premier fisherman of his family. He wears a floppy hat that's L.L. Bean–style, only flashier. He baits up, has a couple of beers, catches a fifteen-inch striper, and says, "I should throw him back. It's not legal to keep stripers under sixteen inches, but he was hooked so deep, he'd die. I won't throw him in the bucket—just leave him on the ground next to it. That way, if the game warden comes, I'll just say, 'Don't ask me—it's not my fish. Somebody leave the fish laying there.' The game warden comes down here sometimes. Man in khaki pants and shirt. Sometimes he waits up in the parking lot on the other side of the tracks to catch people leaving with fish. Fifty-dollar fine if he catch you.

"Best bait for stripers is bloodworms. They cost two-fifty a dozen, and you have to use the whole worm. Catching big fish is too expensive. Best place to fish for stripers is up from here, by the sugar plant. Stripers love sugar. All of those tanks up at the sugar plant are full of syrup. It's really thick—you can't drink it. But if you can sneak in there at night and get some syrup out of those tanks, it makes a good medicine mixed with tea when you get a cold.

"Biggest striper I ever caught here was eight pounds. Biggest striper I ever saw caught here was twelve pounds. Once, I caught a five-pound striper with a tag on it. The tag said to mail the size of the striper, the weight, the place caught, and the day caught to this address in Albany and they'd send me five dollars. I wrote them last week and said, 'I got the striper. You send me the five dollars and I'll tell you anything else you want.'

"I catch stripers, perch, snappers here. Over by City Island, in Long Island Sound, I catch porgies, flounders, and big blue-fish. Once I was fishing for bluefish with a friend of mine on Randalls Island across from the state prison hospital, and we were using big hooks and sixty-pound-test line, and my friend hooked something and it was really big but we could pull it in because the current was with us, and when we got it up, it was a dead guy. He had tried to swim away from the prison and escape two days before. He was dressed—didn't have any shoes on. We called the police."

(1980)

AN ANGLER AT HEART

Often during the past seven years, I have taken a walk from the offices of *The New Yorker* along Forty-third Street—across Fifth Avenue, across Madison Avenue, across Vanderbilt Avenue—then through Grand Central Terminal, across Lexington Avenue, up to Forty-fourth Street, into the elevator at 141 East Forty-fourth Street, up to the third floor, and through the belled door of a small fishing-tackle shop called the Angler's Roost, whose sole proprietor is a man named Jim Deren. Since I've been taking this walk, the Biltmore Men's Bar, which I used to pass at the corner of Madison and Forty-third, changed to the Biltmore Bar, which then became a different bar, named the Café Fanny, which was replaced by a computer store called Digital's, which moved (along with a lot of other stores on the block) after the Biltmore Hotel closed and disappeared under renovators' scaffolding. Once, on this walk, I had to detour around some barricades inside Grand Central, because a film crew was working on the movie *Superman*. Valerie Perrine and Gene Hackman were supposedly there, but I did not see them. Since then, I have seen the movie in a theater and have noted the part that the crew must have been working on when I passed by. During these seven years, the huge Kodak display in the station near the Lexington Avenue wall, which people say ruins the station's interior light and makes it difficult to distinguish the beautiful Venetian-summer-night starscape on the ceiling, has featured photographs of water-skiers behind motorboats, a Bicentennial celebration with men dressed as Continental soldiers, the Pyramid of the Sun at Teotihuacán (by night, lighted), the opening ceremonies of the Winter Olympics at Lake Placid, the Great Wall of China, and, one spring, a close-up shot of a robin, which looked frightening at that size. One time, I came in through the door at Forty-third Street and there before me, across the echoing well of the concourse, was a view of a rock-cluttered desert, barn red under a pink sky, with a little piece of the foot of a space probe visible in the foreground—Mars, photographed by Viking 2.

A fisherman can look at some sections of any trout stream clean enough for fish to live in and say with confidence, A large fish lives there. The water should be deep, and it should be well aerated; that is, it should be free-flowing, rich in oxygen, and not stagnant. There should be a source of food: a grassy bank with beetles, grasshoppers, field mice, and frogs; or a little tributary creek with minnows, chubs, dace, and sculpins; or an upstream section with a silt bottom for large, burrowing mayfly nymphs. There should be cover—downed logs, overhanging tree branches, undercut banks. Where these conditions are found, the chances are very good that at least one large fish will be found as well. Such sections of a river are called good lies. A good lie will usually have a good fish lying in wait, gently finning, looking upstream for whatever the current may bring him.

I have always thought that, as lies go, it would be hard to find a better one than Grand Central Terminal. It is deep—water that deep would be a dark blue. Aerated streams of humanity cascade down the escalators from the Pan Am Building, and flow from the rest of midtown, the rest of the city, the rest of the world, through trains and subways and airport buses and taxis, into its deep pool and out again, and the volume of this flow makes it rich in the important nutrient called capital. Well, in this good lie, the big fish of the fishing-tackle business is Jim Deren, of the Angler's Roost. For over forty years he has had a shop in the area—a shop that has outlasted changes in fishing fashions, changes in the economy, competitors who gave their shops names intentionally similar to his, and finally even Abercrombie & Fitch, his biggest local competitor, which closed its midtown store in 1977. All this time, Deren has remained in his good lie, gently finning behind the counter in his shop, consulting with fishermen from just about every place where there's water, selling every kind of angling supply imaginable, taking in cash and checks as gracefully as a big brown trout sips mayflies from the surface of a Catskill stream.

The first time I met Jim Deren, I was looking for a particular dry fly (a pattern called the Gold-Ribbed Hare's Ear, with a body that goes all the way back over the bend of the hook), which had worked well for me in Wyoming and which I could not find anywhere. I came across the entry for the Angler's Roost in the Yellow Pages:

ANGLER'S ROOST
FISHING TECHNICIANS
Tackle, Salt & Fresh, Lures, Flies
Fly Materials, Waders & Clothing
Repairs, Books & Advertising Props
JIM DEREN ADVISOR

That impressed me. I called the shop one Saturday afternoon around six o'clock and was surprised to find Deren there. In later years, I have learned that he is in his shop at all hours: I have found him in at seven-fifteen on a beautiful Sunday evening in June; I have found him in on all sorts of holidays, when midtown is nothing but blowing papers. On that first Saturday Deren told me that he was about to go home but that if I came in soon he would wait for me. I arrived at the shop half an hour later. He did not happen to have the exact fly I wanted, but he told me where to get it. We talked for a while, and I left without buying anything—the only time that has ever happened.

A few months later, during a really warm April, I decided I had to go fishing, even though I had never been fishing in the East and knew nothing about it. I bought a fishing license at the Department of Environmental Conservation office on the sixty-first floor of the World Trade Center, and then I went to see Deren. He told me the book to buy—*New Streamside Guide to Naturals and Their Imitations*, by Art Flick. He said that, because it had been so warm, certain mayflies that would usually be on the stream later in the season might have already appeared. He sold me flies imitating those insects. He told me where to fish—in the Beaverkill, the Little Beaverkill, and Willowemoc Creek, near Roscoe, New York. He told me what bus to take. I left his shop, went back to my apartment, got my fly rod and sleeping bag, went to the Port Authority Bus Terminal, boarded a Short Line bus, and rode for two and a half hours with Hasidic Jews going to Catskill resorts and women going to upstate ashrams. On the bus I read the *Streamside Guide*, which says that mayflies live for several years underwater as swimming nymphs, hatch into winged insects, mate while hovering over the water, lay their eggs in the water, and die; that recently hatched mayflies, called duns, float along the surface and are easy for trout to catch, and so are the stage of the mayfly's life cycle most sensible for the angler to imitate with artificials; that different species of mayflies hatch at different times of the year, according to water temperature; and that the different species emerge every year in an order so invariable as to be the only completely predictable aspect of trout fishing. I got off the bus in Roscoe about four in the afternoon, walked to the Beaverkill, hid my sleeping bag in some willows, set up my fly rod, and walked up the river until I reached a spot with no fishermen. I noticed mayflies in the air, noticed dragonflies zipping back and forth eating the mayflies. I saw a dragonfly pick a mayfly out of the air so neatly that he took only the body, leaving the two wings to flutter down to the surface of the stream and float away. I caught a mayfly myself after a lot of effort, compared it with the pictures in my *Streamside Guide*, decided that it was the male of the *Ephemerella subvaria* (Deren had been right; according to the book, that insect wasn't due for about two weeks more), tied on its imitation (a pattern called the Red Quill, in size 14), made a short cast, caught a little trout, made a few more short casts, caught another little trout, and waited while a fat guy with a spinning rod who said he wasn't having much luck walked by me up the river. Then I made a good, long cast under a spruce bough to a patch of deep water ringed with lanes of current, like a piece of land in the middle of a circular freeway-access ramp. This patch of water had a smooth, tense surface marked with little tucks where eddying water was boiling up from underneath. My fly sat motionless on this water for a time that when I replay it in my mind seems really long. Then a fish struck so hard it was like a person punching up through the water with his fist. Water splashed several feet in the air, and there was a flash of fish belly of that particular shade of white—like the white of a horse's eye when it's scared, or the white of the underside of poplar leaves blown by wind right before a storm—that often seems to accompany violence in nature. The fish ran downstream like crazy (I don't remember setting the hook), then he ran upstream, then he ran downstream again. He jumped several times—not arched and poised, as in the sporting pictures, but flapping back and forth so fast he was a blur. Line was rattling in my line guides; I was pulling it in and he was taking it out, until finally there was a big pile of line at my feet, and the fish, also, in the shallow water at my feet. He was a thirteen-inch brook trout, with a wild eye that was a circle of black set in a circle of gold. The speckles on his back reproduced the wormlike marks on the rocks on the stream bottom, and his sides were filled with colors—orange, red, silver, purple, midnight blue—and yet were the opposite of gaudy. I hardly touched him; he was lightly hooked. I released him, and after a short while he swam away. I stood for maybe ten minutes, with my fly rod lying on the gray, softball-sized rocks, and I stared at the trees on the other side of the river. The feeling was like having hundreds of gag hand-buzzers applied to my entire body.

Since that day I have always loved the Red Quill dry fly, and particularly the Red Quill that Deren sells, which is the most elegant I have ever seen. For me, the Red Quill is a shamanistic medicine bundle that called forth the strike, the flash of belly, the living palette of colors from that spring day, and years later, even in situations where it is not remotely the right fly, I find myself tying it on just to see what will happen.

Also since that day I have believed that Jim Deren is a great man. He is the greatest man I know of who will talk to just anybody off the street.

In appearance, Deren is piscine. He is stocky—probably about five feet ten inches tall. His hair is in a mouse-brown brush cut, about half an inch long. His forehead is corrugated with several distinct wrinkles, which run up and down, like marks of soil erosion on a hill. His eyes are weak and watery and blue, behind thick glasses with thick black frames. There is a large amount of what looks like electrical tape around the glasses at the bridge. His eyebrows are cinnamon-colored. His nose is thick, and his lips are thick. He has a white mustache. His direct, point-blank regard can be unsettling. People who have fished their whole lives sometimes find themselves saying when they encounter this gaze that they don't know a thing about fishing, really. Deren has a style of garment which he loves and which he wears almost every single day in his shop. This garment is the jumpsuit. For a long time, he wore either a charcoal-gray jumpsuit or an olive-green jumpsuit. One or both of the jumpsuits had a big ring on the zipper at the throat. Recently, Deren has introduced another jumpsuit into the repertoire. This is a sky-blue jumpsuit with a green-on-white emblem of a leaping bass on the left breast pocket. Deren's voice is deep and gravelly. I can do a good imitation of him. The only sentence I can think of that might make his accent audible on paper (in the last word, anyway) is one I have heard him speak several times while he was talking on one of his unfavorite topics, the "flower children": "In late October, early November, when we're driving back from fishing out West, with the wind howling and huge dark snow clouds behind us, sometimes we pass these frail girls, these flower children, standing by the side of the road in *shawwwwwwwwwls*."

I say Deren is probably about five feet ten inches tall because even though he often says, "I've been running around all day. I'm exhausted," I have actually seen him standing up only a few times. Like a psychiatrist, Deren is usually seated. I have seen him outside his shop only once—when, as I was leaving, he came down in the elevator to pick up a delivery on the first floor. (Ambulant, he seemed to me surprisingly nimble.) It is appropriate for Deren to be seated all the time, because he has tremendous repose. There is a lot of bad repose going around these days: the repose of someone watching a special Thursday-night edition of *Monday Night Football*; the repose of someone smoking a cigarette on a ten-minute break at work; the repose of driving; the repose of waiting in line at the bank. Deren is in his sixties. The fish he has caught, the troubles he has been through, the fishing tackle he has sold, the adventures he has had lend texture to his repose. On good days, his repose hums like a gyroscope.

Deren talking about the Angler's Roost while sitting in his shop on a slow afternoon in March: "It seems only natural that I would have gravitated to this business. I've been tying flies ever since I was in short pants. When I was in grade school in New Jersey, I used to go without lunch because I wanted to save my money and buy fishing tackle. I remember fashioning a fly from a jacket of mine when I was a kid just barely big enough to be let out of sight. I tied it out of a lumber jacket that my mother had made for me—"

The phone rings.

"Hello. Angler's Roost."

". . . . ."

"Christ, I don't know a thing about Chinese trout fishing, Doc."

". . . . ."

"Well, they gotta have trout fishing. The Japanese have trout fishing. Just the other day, I sold some stuff to Yasuo Yoshida, the Japanese zipper magnate. He's probably got more tackle than I got. He's *kichi* about trout fishing. *Kichi*—that's Japanese for nuts."

". . . . ."

"Well, I think the Russians should open one or two of their rivers for salmon fishing, certainly. They just have to have terrific salmon fishing."

". . . . ."

"Look at it this way—next time you'll know."

". . . . ."

"Whatever you find out, Doc, let me know when you get back. Have a good time.

"Anyway, I had this blue-gray lumber jacket, and there was this little blue fly on the water. The goddamn fish weren't considering anything but this fly. Well, between the lining and the thread of my jacket, I made a fly that looked something like the insect, and so, glory be, after some effort I caught a fish. The fish made a mistake, and that did it. This was on a little stream in Pennsylvania, a little tributary of the Lehigh. It was a day as miserable as this, but later in the year."

Deren picks up a package of Keebler Iced Oatmeal and Raisin Cookies, breaks it open in the middle, and dumps all the contents into a white plastic quart bucket—the kind of bucket that ice cream comes in. He starts to eat the cookies.

"After that, I was really hooked. I collected all kinds of items for fly-tying. Cigarette and cigar wrappers, hairs from dogs. Christ, I cut hair off every goddamn thing that was around. Picked up feathers in pet shops. I was always raiding chickens or ducks. I remember I tried to get some feathers from some geese and they ran me the hell out the county. Horsetails. Anything. It wasn't long before I was selling some of the flies I tried. As far as I know, I was the first commercial nymph-tier in the country. I was selling flies in New York, New Jersey, and fairly deep into Pennsylvania. Fishing was a great thing for me, now that I look back on it, because in a lot of the contact sports I was always busting my glasses. But row a boat—I had a pair of chest muscles, looked like a goddamn weight lifter. I was very well coordinated. I had coordination and timing. That has something to do with fishing. I was a good wing shot."

Deren reaches under the counter and produces a banana. With a table knife he cuts the banana in half. He eats one half and leaves the other half, in the skin, on top of a pile of papers. Later, a customer will find in the pile of papers a copy of a fishing magazine that he has been looking for. He will take it out from under the half banana and buy it.

"I spent all my time in high school fishing, and one day I noticed this guy was watching me. He'd been watching me a few times before. He'd ask me questions. Well, it turned out this guy had a radio show about fishing and hunting. I think he called himself Bill the Fisherman. He started telling people about me—called me the Child Fisherman Prodigy. He told the proprietor of a fishing-tackle shop in the heart of Newark, right by Penn Station, and the man hired me, and eventually I became the youngest fishing-tackle buyer in the country. Not long after that, I was imported by an outfit in New York called Alex Taylor & Company, on Forty-second Street. I put them in the fishing-tackle business—"

The phone rings again.

"Angler's Roost."

". . . . ."

"We've got all kinds of hook hones."

". . . . ."

"Fresh and salt, both."

". . . . ."

"Yes, some of them are grooved."

". . . . ."

"Two different grooves."

". . . . ."

"Each one comes in a plastic case."

". . . . ."

"Different lengths. I think two-inch and three-inch."

". . . . ."

"What the hell do you mean, who makes it? It's a goddamn hook hone! What the hell difference does it make who makes it?

"Guy wants to know who makes the hook hone. Wants to know what *brand* it is. Christ. Anyway, after that I became a buyer and salesman for another house, called Kirtland Brothers, downtown. They're now extinct. I advised their clients on the technical aspects of fly-fishing. Mainly, I handled their fly-tying material. About this time, I began my mail-order business, selling fly-tying material through ads in different magazines. I was working all day for Kirtland Brothers, then staying up all night to handle my mail orders. Finally, it got unmanageable as a side business. I wasn't doing justice to either job. I finished my obligations to that firm, and then I opened up the first Angler's Roost, at 207 East Forty-third, above where the Assembly Restaurant used to be. I dreamed up the name myself. You had the roost connotation because it was up off the street and you had guys that hung around all day with the eternal bull sessions. (I was thinking of selling coffee and cake there for a while.) Then you think of birds roosting, and of course, a lot of what we sold was feathers. And a lot of the feathers were rooster feathers—capes and necks."

Deren takes from the pocket of his jumpsuit a new pack of True Blue cigarettes. With a fly-tying bodkin, he makes a number of holes all the way through the pack. Then he takes out a cigarette and lights it.

"Since its inception, the Roost has been tops in its field. We've had every kind of customer, from the bloated bondholder to the lowliest form of human life. Frank Jay Gould, the son of the railroad magnate, once bought a boat over my telephone. Ted Williams used to stop by whenever the Red Sox were in town. He was a saltwater fisherman, but we infected him with the salmon bug. We've had boxers, bandleaders, diplomats, ambassadors. Benny Goodman used to come in all the time. I sold Artie Shaw his salmon outfit. So many notable people, I don't even remember. Engelhard, of Engelhard precious metals. Marilyn Monroe's photographer, Milton Greene. Señor Wences—the ventriloquist who did the thing with the box. Bing Crosby. Tex Ritter. He was an uncle of mine by my first marriage; I got a lot of other customers in

Nashville through him. We've had more than one President. Eisenhower came in once. He was a nice guy—didn't have his nose too far up in the air. We've had three generations of people come in here, maybe four. We've had some of the very elite. A lot of them don't want their names mentioned."

Deren looks left, cocks his wrist as if he were throwing a dart, and flips the cigarette out of sight behind the counter.

"We had our own television show, which ran for twenty-six weeks on the old DuMont Television Network. It was called *The Sportsman's Guide*. It was sponsored by Uhu Glue—a miracle glue, kind of like Krazy Glue. The announcer was a guy named Connie Evans. I did the lecturing—like on a spinning reel—and then when we did a fishing trip I did the fishing. That television show wasn't on very long before people started calling me Uncle Jimmy. I don't know how it got started, but it stuck. I was also a technical panelist on a radio show called *The Rod and Gun Club of the Air*. The other panelists and I shot the breeze amongst us every week."

A blond woman in a beige knit ski cap comes in. She asks Deren if he has an eight-foot bamboo fly rod. He says he doesn't but he can order one for her. The woman says, "Oh, that's great. I think he might marry me if I find him that rod." She leaves.

"Did I tell you about our television show? *The Sportsman's Guide*? Did I tell you about our heavy involvement in the advertising field? Over the years we've acted as consultant on hundreds and hundreds of ads. Sooner or later, everybody uses a fishing ad. Also, the slogan 'How's your love life?' started in the Roost. I used to ask my customers that when they came in, and then it became the slogan for a brand of toothpaste.

"We developed the first satisfactory big-game reel—the

Penn 12/0 Senator. I guess there's six or seven miles of those things now. We also helped develop the concept of R and R— Rest and Recuperation—for the military. The idea was to take these guys who'd been through the horrors of war, get them fishing, get them fly-tying, get their minds off their former troubles. Some of the stuff I wrote on fly-tying for the Navy was posted in battleships that are now in mothballs. We also supplied the cord that made Dracula's wings move, for the Broadway show. We've always been an international business. Anglers come from India, Australia, New Zealand, Tasmania, Norway, Iceland, Ireland, Holland, Germany, France, Italy, Switzerland, Canada, Mexico, South Africa, South America— so many South Americans you'd think it was just next door, and they're all loaded. Bolivia, Tierra del Fuego. Any guy who's a nut about a fly comes to the Roost eventually. Anyplace a trout swims, they know the Roost. Not only trout. Also bonefish, tarpon, sailfish, striped bass, salmon—"

The phone rings again.

"Angler's Roost."

". . . . ."

"Hello, my little pigeon."

". . . . ."

"Just a few minutes. I'm leaving right now."

In Deren's shop, three customers can stand comfortably. You can stand and put your hands in your pockets, but there really isn't room to move around much. Four is tight. Five is cr   '. Six is very crowded. When there are six customers   ⁿ, one of them has to hold on to somebody to keep   over backward into the knee-high wader bin. Except for the small space around the customers' feet, Deren's shop is 360 degrees of fishing equipment, camping equipment, books, and uncategorizable stuff. The shop is like a forest in that if you remain silent in either of them for any length of time you will hear something drop.

"What the hell was that?"

"I think it was a book."

"Don't worry about it. Leave it there."

"*Better Badminton?* Jim, how come you have a book called *Better Badminton?*"

"A lot of these things get shipped by mistake, and then it's too goddamn much trouble to send them back."

In Deren's shop, he has tackle for the three different kinds of sportfishing—bait casting, spin fishing, and fly-fishing. Bait-casting outfits are the standard rod and reel that cartoonists usually give to fishermen. The reel has a movable spool, and both rod and reel are designed for bait or for lures heavy enough to be cast with their own weight. Spin-fishing rods and reels are also designed for lures heavy enough to be cast with their own weight, but because of refinements in the reel—a nonmovable spool that allows the line to spiral off— spin-fishing rods cast farther with less weight. In fly-fishing, the lure is usually nothing but feathers on a hook, so it does not have enough weight to be cast. Fly-fishing equipment con- sists of longer, lighter rods and a thick, tapered line, which work together with a whipping action to cast the fly. All three of these kinds of fishing can be done in either fresh or salt wa- ter. The sea is bigger than the land; saltwater tackle is usually bigger and heavier than freshwater tackle. Deren sells saltwa- ter rods as thick as mop handles, and freshwater fly rods like Seiji Ozawa's baton. They are made of bamboo, fiberglass, metal, or (recent developments) graphite or boron. He sells reels like boat winches, and palm-sized reels that sound like Swiss watches when you crank them. He has thousands of miles of line—nylon monofilament or braided nylon or plastic or braided Dacron or silk or wire. He has hooks from size 28, which are small enough to fit about five on a fingertip, to size 16/0, which have a four-inch gap between the point of the hook and the shank.

Deren also has:

thousands of lures designed to imitate live game-fish prey, with names like Bass-Oreno, Original Spin-Oreno, Buzz'n Cobra, Chugger, Lucky 13, Crazy Crawler, Hopkins No-Eql, Goo-Goo Eyes, Hula Popper, Jitterbug, Devil's Horse, Creek Chub Wiggle Fish, Flatfish, Lazy Ike, Red Eye, Dardevle, Fluke Slayer, Ava Diamond Jig, Rapala, Dancing Doll Jig, Rebel, Darter, Mirrolure, Shyster, Abu-Reflex, Swedish Wobbler, Hawaiian Wiggler, Golden-Eye Troublemaker, Hustler, Al's Goldfish, Pikie Minnow, Salty Shrimper, Williams Wobbler, Tiny Tad, Tiny Torpedo, Zara (named after Zarragossa Street, the former red-light district in Pensacola, Florida, because of its attractive wiggle);

countless trout flies that imitate mayflies at every stage of their life, with names like Quill Gordon, Hendrickson, March Brown, Red Quill, Grey Fox, Lady Beaverkill, Light Cahill, Grey Fox Variant, Dun Variant, Cream Variant, Blue-Winged Olive, Sulphur Dun, Brown Drake, Green Drake, Pale Evening Dun, Little White-Winged Black;

trout flies that imitate other insects—the Letort Hopper, Jassid, Black Ant, Red Ant, Cinnamon Ant, Black Gnat, Spider, Leaf Roller, Stonefly, Caddis, Case Caddis, Caddis Worm, Caddis Pupa, Dragonfly, Hellgrammite, Damselfly;

flies that imitate mice, frogs, and bats;

streamer flies—the Muddler Minnow, Spruce Fly, Spuddler,

Professor, Supervisor, Black Ghost, Grey Ghost, Mickey Finn—which are probably meant to imitate minnows;

other flies—the Parmachenee Belle, Lord Baltimore, Yellow Sally, Adams, Rat-Faced McDougal, Woolly Worm, Hare's Ear, Humpy, Royal Coachman, Hair-Wing Royal Coachman, Lead-Wing Coachman, Queen of the Waters, Black Prince, Red Ibis—of which it is hard to say just what they are supposed to imitate, and which are sometimes called attractor flies;

big, colorful salmon flies, with names like Nepisiquit, Abbey, Thunder and Lightning, Amherst, Black Fairy, Orange Blossom, Silver Doctor, Dusty Miller, Hairy Mary, Lancelot, Jock Scott, Fair Duke, Durham Ranger, Marlodge, Fiery Brown, Night Hawk, Black Dose, Warden's Worry;

flies that he invented himself—Deren's Stonefly, Deren's Fox, Deren's Harlequin, The Fifty Degrees, The Torpedo, The Black Beauty, Deren's Speckled Caddis, Deren's Cream Caddis, Deren's Cinnamon Caddis, Deren's Grey Caddis;

feathers for tying flies—rooster (domestic and foreign, winter plumage and summer plumage, dozens of shades), ostrich, goose, kingfisher, mallard, peacock, turkey, imitation jungle cock, imitation marabou, imitation wood duck;

fur—Alaskan seal, arctic fox, mink, beaver, weasel, imitation chinchilla, raccoon, ermine, rabbit, fitch, marten, gray fox, skunk, squirrel, civet cat—also for tying flies;

hair—deer, bear, antelope, moose, goat, elk, badger, calf—also for tying flies;

scissors, forceps, pliers, razors, vises, lamps, tweezers, bobbins, bodkins, floss, thread, chenille, tinsel, Mylar, lead wire, wax, yarn—also for tying flies;

chest waders, wader suspenders, wader belts, wader cleats, wader racks, wader patch kits, wading shoes, wading staffs, hip boots, boot dryers, inner boot soles, Hijack brand V-notch boot removers, insulated socks, fishing vests, bug-repellent fishing vests, rain pants, ponchos, head nets, long-billed caps, hunting jackets, thermal underwear, high-visibility gloves, fishing shirts; ice augers, dried grasshoppers, minnow scoops, fish stringers, hook disgorgers, rubber casting weights, gigs, spears, car-top rod carriers, rubber insect legs, fish-tank aerators, English game bags, wicker creels, folding nets, hand gaffs, worm rigs, gasoline-motor starter cords, watercolor paintings of the Miramichi River, sponge-rubber bug bodies, line straighteners, knot-tiers, snakebite kits, hatbands, leather laces, salmon eggs, plastic-squid molds, stuff you spray on your glasses so they won't fog up, duck and crow calls, waterproof match cases, lead split-shot, collapsible oars, bells that you hook up to your line so they ring when a fish takes your bait, Justrite electric head lanterns, dried mayfly nymphs, rescue whistles, canteens, butterfly nets, peccary bristles, porcupine quills, frog harnesses . . .

The truth is, I have no idea of all the things Deren has in his shop. Just about every item he sells is appropriate to a particular angling situation. In addition to the part of the shop that the customer sees, the Angler's Roost fills a couple of large back rooms, a lot of space in an office on another floor of the same building, and space that Deren rents in a warehouse in New Jersey. I have not yet encountered, nor would I encounter in several lifetimes of angling, all the different situations for which the different items in his shop are intended.

Deren likes to recite certain fishing maxims over and over, and although he says his intent is purely educational ("We don't sell anybody. We advise, and then they do their own buying") I have seen his maxims work on customers' wallets the way oyster knives work on oysters. One of these maxims is "Ninety percent of a trout's diet consists of food he finds underwater." A customer who hears this often decides he has to have a couple dozen stone-fly nymphs—weighted flies that imitate the nymphal stage of the stone fly, an insect common in rocky streambeds. The stone fly that Deren sells is two dollars, which makes it one of the more expensive trout flies he sells. Another maxim is "Trout don't always see a floating mayfly from underneath; when a trout is taking a fly he will break the surface"—here Deren does an imitation of a trout regarding with bulging eye a fly at eye level—"and when he does he sees that the back of the insect is darkly vermiculated." A customer who hears this may conclude that he cannot be without several flies—in the pattern called Deren's Fox, as it happens—that have across the back a number of stripes made with a bodkin dipped in lacquer, to suggest the dark vermiculations. (Deren's imitation of a trout breaking the surface and seeing a fly is itself worth the price of a lot of Deren's Foxes.) Another maxim is "People always say that a fly reel is nothing more than a storage case for line, but this is not true. A fly reel has many functions it must perform. It has to be the right weight, it has to be the right size to hold the proper amount of line, and it has to have a smooth drag"—the mechanism that controls the amount of resistance offered to a fish pulling line off the reel—"which can be adjusted to the various situations you may encounter." Another maxim, one of Deren's most serviceable, which often comes up when a customer is contemplating an unusually expensive purchase, is "The money may not seem worth it, but when you run across a fish you've waited your whole life to catch and then lose him because your equipment was substandard—well, then the money becomes immaterial."

One spring, just before I was going to Key West to visit my grandmother, Deren got me in the pincers of the last two maxims as I was deciding on a new fly reel: people say a fly reel is just a storage case for line but you need a good reel with a good drag, etc.; and if you buy a substandard (i.e., cheaper) reel and because of it lose the fish of your life, etc. I was planning to wade the tidal flats around the islands fly-fishing for bonefish and permit (a kind of pompano), of which the first is supposed to be very difficult to catch and the second is supposed to be about impossible to catch. Like a lot of people before me and after me, I cracked. I spent $110 on an English-made reel with level adjustable drag, which came in a fleece-lined suede case. The first day, I fished with it at a fishing spot that had been recommended by a guy behind the counter at a bait-and-tackle shop called Boog Powell's Anglers Marine (it is owned by the former baseball star, but I have never seen him in there), on Stock Island, the key just up from Key West. This fishing spot was a long sandbar behind the Boca Chica Naval Air Station, the military installation that sometimes used to appear on TV as a piece of runway and an airplane wing and some heat shimmers in the background of news stories about Cuban refugees. My cousin dropped me off there. She had to take the car back to get the seats reupholstered. (My grandmother spends a lot of time driving people in wet bathing suits around, so her seat covers always fall apart.) I hid my lunch, which my grandmother had packed for me, in the mangroves. Black mangroves, since they grow in or near water, have hundreds of little breathing tubes that aerate their roots and look like Bic pen tops sticking up from the mud. As I waded out, I scared up a couple of shore birds, which made regularly spaced splashes with their feet on the surface of the water as they took off. The sandbar, a line of white between turquoise water and dark-blue water, was maybe a quarter mile out. I had to wade in up to my armpits at one point. I was nervous. I had never heard of a wading angler being eaten by a shark, but I didn't know why. It seemed as if anything that wanted to come in and get me could. At one point I almost stepped on a ray, which stirred up big clouds of mud as it winged away. I was doubly scared when I realized that my fear was probably releasing chemicals into the water which would call predators in from all over the ocean. On the sandbar, the water was ankle-deep. I worked my way along, casting to the deep water on the ocean side of the bar. It was very windy, and I kept hitting myself between the shoulder blades with the weighted fly when I cast. I saw one fish over the half mile of sandbar that I covered. I'm not sure what kind of fish it was—I don't think it was a permit or a bonefish. It was about two feet long. It wasn't expecting to find anybody standing in the water out there. About ten feet from me, it saw me, and it did the closest thing to a double take I've ever seen a fish do. Then it disappeared like the Road Runner in the cartoon, with a ricochet noise. I waded back to shore, stepping on crunching white coral and then slogging through a long patch of grayish-white ooze—the kind of muck that dinosaurs left footprints in. I was quite a distance from where I'd left my lunch. I began to walk back along the road. As I came around a bend in the road, I saw a camper parked. It had Alabama license plates. About the same time I saw the camper, I heard the jingle of a dog collar. With one bark, a Great Dane plunged out of the bushes toward me. A second later, a dachshund and a border collie, both barking a lot, came out of the bushes. The Great Dane came up to my shoulder, and had a mouth—filled with yellow, pointed teeth—that could have eaten a clock radio. A man and a woman were sunbathing on deck chairs near the camper. The man did not get up. The woman told me to hold still and the dog wouldn't bite me. I held still, and the dog bit me in the right shoulder. I told the woman that the dog was biting me. The border collie was nipping around my knees, the dachshund around my ankles. The Great Dane bit me in the right buttock. The woman was putting on her sandals. The Great Dane bit me hard next to my left shoulder blade. The woman came up and pulled him off. I walked a distance away, and then I raised my shirt and turned my back to the woman and asked her if I was bleeding. She said I wasn't. I walked on up the road. The dachshund continued to nip around my ankles for a way up the road. The woman was calling him. His name was Fritz. I got to the place in the mangroves where I'd left my lunch, and I found my lunch and sat down on a mangrove root. My shirt was not torn where the dog had bitten me in the right shoulder, and my pants weren't torn where the dog had bitten me in the right buttock. But the lower back of my shirt was torn, with several long tooth holes. I felt my back. I had two puncture wounds, and they were bleeding. I walked back to where the camper had been parked, shouting for the people to hold the dog. The camper was not there anymore. (I later found out that the state of Florida requires that anytime a dog bites a person it must be locked up for ten days to see if it has rabies. The Alabamians, possibly having had this kind of experience before, and not wanting to change their vacation plans, may have left the minute I was out of sight.) I ate my lunch and thought about what I should do. I decided that the dog probably did not have rabies but was just crazy and overbred, like many Great Danes. I decided that it would not be worth it to try to get back to Key West—that it made more sense to wait for my cousin to come and pick me up. I wasn't going to bleed to death. I went back out and fished some more, seeing this time not a single fish. However, I did spot a yellow object floating by me and snagged it with my rod, and the object turned out to be a plastic toy man—part of the Fisher-Price toy dump truck recommended for ages two to six. I put it in my pocket, because at that time my cousin's daughter really liked Fisher-Price toys. I kept hearing voices shouting back and forth along the shore. When my cousin finally blew the horn for me and I went in, I learned that the voices had belonged, probably, to whoever had been engaged in stringing coils of barbed wire along the shoreline. (Probably it was the Seabees putting out the wire for airfield security.) This barbed wire had barbs on it shaped like little meat cleavers. I made it through the first two coils, but I got tangled up in the third coil, cutting my legs in several places. When I got to the car and dismantled my fly rod, I broke off a line guide. My cousin's daughter was with her, and she was very happy with the Fisher-Price man I'd found. My cousin took me to the de Poo Hospital, in Key West, where a twenty-nine-year-old doctor with long hair, from Chillicothe, Ohio, who had decided to practice in Key West because he hated the winters in Ohio, told me that there hadn't been a case of rabies in Florida in a really long time and that house dogs like Great Danes almost never got rabies anyway, but that I should have a tetanus shot, so I did, and it cost thirty dollars. I didn't go out fishing, or even think about fishing, for a few days after this, with the result that I forgot to rinse the salt water out of the works of my expensive new reel, with the result that the works corroded to the point where the reel would turn approximately as much as the Chrysler Building turns on its foundation. Now the reel sits on my desk, proving Deren's maxim; more than a storage case for line, it is also a paperweight.

Although all kinds of people go to Deren's shop, most of his customers are adult white men. This category is large enough to include many subcategories. Some of these men are technicians; they wear raincoats, gray glen-plaid suits, black-orange-and-yellow-striped ties, and gray plaid Irish walking caps, and the gleam of their metal-rimmed glasses reinforces the expression of scientific curiosity in their eyes. They know no higher words of praise than "state of the art." When Deren shows them the latest graphite fly rod, they ask, "So is this pretty much state of the art in graphite rods?" Others are rich, and probably social. They bring with them the warm, Episcopalian smell of Brooks Brothers or the Union Club, and they talk like George Plimpton: "An *English*man who fishes in *Brazil* had this particular kind of *lanyard*, do you know the kind I mean, *marvelous*, yes, that's exactly what I want, yes, *good* for you!" Others are writers or photographers or painters; they are quiet or loud, hungover or not hungover, and many of them carry shoulder bags and don't wear suits and look as if somebody had smudged them when they were wet. Others are short, bluff, bald men who look like walking thumbs and laugh after every sentence they speak; sometimes they open the door and yell, "Hey, mister! Got any hooks?" and then they laugh delightedly. Others are terse. That's what they do for a living. They're professionally terse: "Jim. Ask you a question. Winchester. Model 21. Twenty-gauge." Others are executives in the oil business who are leaving tomorrow for

Bahrain. Once, I heard the executives in the elevator going up to Deren's talking about the management characteristics of different oil companies. One of them said that top management at Mobil Oil suffered from "paralysis by analysis." Others are big, wear size 11 shoes, have red faces, and come into the shop in the afternoon with cocktails and good lunch on their breath, and shoot the bull with Deren for hours.

Guy: "Jimmy, let me ask you something and you tell me what you think of this. Last August I was sitting on the bank of a river in Michigan waiting for it to cool off and for the fish to start feeding, and I saw this white thing bouncing along the river bottom, and when it got close enough I saw that it was a peeled potato, and when it came closer I saw that a twelve- or thirteen-inch trout was *bouncing* the potato along the river bottom with his nose—"

Deren: "You sure it was a potato?"

Guy: "It was either a peeled potato or maybe a peeled apple. This trout was bouncing it; I swear, he was dribbling it with his nose along the bottom like a ball. Friend of mine and I followed him downstream a long way. He just kept dribbling that potato. Now, what in the hell could that have been?"

Deren: "I don't know. I've never seen a trout do anything like that. But that reminds me—did I ever tell you about the time I saved a trout from drowning? The reason it reminds me is that I saw the trout bouncing and flopping along the bottom with the current. Good-sized brook trout. I caught up with him and netted him, and I discovered that he had a caddis case—you know, the protective covering that the caddis worm spins around himself, it looks kind of like a twig—well, he had one of these caddis cases, about an inch long, stuck between his upper and lower jaws. It was stuck in his small teeth, so he couldn't close his mouth, and if a trout can't close his mouth he can't filter oxygen through his gills, and he drowns. I took the caddis case out, and I put the trout in some shallow water, and pretty soon, proud as beans, he swam away."

Guy: "I was reading in some sporting magazine about a man who was fishing in a boat and he had his retriever dog with him, and as he made a cast he accidentally let go of the rod and it flew out into the lake, and the dog immediately jumped in after it, and he started swimming to shore and the lure was trailing in the water, and a fish hit the lure, and the dog kept on swimming, and he ran up on the shore and kept on running until he'd pulled the fish all the way out of the water."

Deren: "Could happen. Could happen. I remember once I was out in a boat casting a deer-hair bug for bass, and my leader was frayed, and when a big bass hit I broke the bug off in his mouth, so I put on a new leader and continued to fish, and then a couple of hours later I decided to quit fishing, and I was coming back to the dock, and suddenly there was an enormous splash next to the boat and this big bass came out of the water into the air and landed in the bottom of my boat. It was the same fish I'd hooked earlier—he still had my lure in his jaw. Of course, there's a simple explanation. The fish was jumping trying to throw the lure. He would probably have kept at it until he succeeded, but instead he landed in my boat."

Guy: "That doesn't surprise me. Did I ever tell you about the time . . ."

Other customers are men of considerable personal force, but when they come into Deren's shop Deren is sitting, they are standing; Deren knows where everything is, they don't; they are asking, he is telling. After an exchange like "Hi, I'm looking for some leader sink," "Look on that shelf right next to you—no, not there, the other direction. Second shelf. *Second* shelf, that's the third shelf. Move that fly box. Look to the left of that. No, the left. That's the right. Move your hand back where it was going originally. Right there! Right there! It's right in front of you! Look right where your hand is! You're looking right at it," this particular type of customer's ears, having heard more sentences in the imperative mood in the last few seconds than they probably hear in a week, turn pink with embarrassment.

An important customer who has been coming in for many years, or an old fishing buddy, or a fellow angling expert, or any of the guys Deren has got to know over the years, he calls a son of a bitch. If the guy is present, he's "you son of a bitch"; if he's not, he's "that son of a bitch." Deren says the phrase with mastery, with delicate tonal shadings to indicate everything from a wonderful human being to a horrible human being. He says the phrase with the ease of a man turning into his driveway for the ten-thousandth time. When the subject of any one of these guys comes up, Deren will say, "*That* son of a bitch.

—he'll never die, the Devil wouldn't have him."

—he tied saddle hackle on streamer flies with greater intensity than any man I ever knew."

—don't ever let him around a car, he'll destroy it in a second."

—he was a real screwball, a big, tall, good-looking guy. Slept with, lived with, married I don't know how many women."

—did you know he invented the après-ski boot?"

—I've seen drunks dive under the table when he appeared on the scene."

—he's a pinko crêpe-hanger of the first water."

—he married a girl in Greece."

—he's basically a correlator. He's not an originator. He doesn't have spontaneity. Spontaneity is what advances the sport."

—he fathered half the illegitimate children running around [a large American city]."

—he had a compass in his head."

—he would have made a great President, but he wouldn't touch it."

—he could tie flies down to size 28 in his fingers without a vise."

—he was incredible. He'd make bets he could sight a rifle in to zero in three shots. And do it, too."

—he was always into me for something, as well as I knew him."

—he asked me to be the best man at his wedding, and when I got to the wedding he told me to put on my waders, and he was married in a pool on the Ausable River."

—he asked me to sign a bank note for him when he bought a new car, and then he skipped town and I had to pay the bank, and meanwhile, I'm getting these postcards from him, he's out in British Columbia, and he says he's having the best salmon fishing of his life and he wishes I was there!"

—he's a very enthusiastic angler. It's the Indian in him."

—forget it. He's a three-dollar bill. He'd write any kind of angling misinformation he could think of. He prostituted his sport for money. He's not a sportsman."

—he's an enthusiast of an extreme caliber. He won't eat, he won't sleep, he lives by the goddamn tides. This lends him a cloak of irresponsibility, but he is responsible—to the striped bass. He was fishing on the bridge out at Jones Beach, which is illegal, and he had just hooked a big striper when the cops came along, so he jumped over the bridge and hung from the railing with one hand and held all his tackle and played the fish with the other until the cops went away. He's an angler at heart."

In Deren's world, an angler at heart is the best thing you can be. He describes many people as competent anglers or good anglers; he describes some as enthusiastic anglers; only a very few does he describe as anglers at heart. When I asked him what distinguishes the few anglers at heart from the fifty-four million other people who fish in this country, he said, "It's the call of the wild, the instinct of the hunt. It's a throwback to the forest primeval. It's the feeling of being in a state of grace in a magnificent outdoor cathedral. Either you have it or you don't—it's inborn. The first time I went into the woods, it was as if I had been there before." He looked at me significantly.

"You mean . . . like in a previous life?" I asked.

"Well, that would be stretching it. Let's just say I didn't have too many surprises. I could sit all day and watch a field mouse fifteen feet away, watch a bird in a tree huntin' bugs—sometimes they're comical as hell. People would say to me, 'What in the world do you do in the woods that long?' Well, Christ, you never run out of things to do in the woods. The woods are a constant unfolding story. But it wasn't the same if there was anything man-made in view. If you thought of man at all, it was a man who had gone through there silently. Maybe in some long-forgotten time an Indian who went to join his ancestors long before the Norsemen came to the American coast set foot on that same spot when he was following the buffalo. Or maybe it was pristine, the way the Lord of the cathedral made it. The romance of fishing isn't all just fish."

In *The Compleat Angler*, Izaak Walton says, "For Angling is somewhat like poetry, men are to be born so: I mean with inclinations to it, though both may be heightened by discourse and practice, but he that hopes to be a good Angler must not only bring an inquiring, searching, observing wit, but he must bring a large measure of hope and patience, and a love and propensity to the art itself; but having once got and practiced it, then doubt not but Angling will prove to be so pleasant that it will prove to be like virtue, a reward to itself."

More men than women fish. Sometimes this works out fine, but other times the shadow of angry excluded wives and girl-friends falls across the sport, and things get depressing. About women in angling, Deren says, "The Angler's Roost was the first place I know of that trained women. We pioneered in that field. A lot of women were getting fed up with this business of getting left home on the weekends, and so their husbands brought them to us and we trained them. Later on, the women we trained became the nucleus that infected a lot of other women. Of course, you had to indoctrinate them prop-erly. Sit them on a rock and let the bugs chew them up and then ask them if they like it and you're going to get a negative answer. But if you can inculcate the angling mystique into them, you've got yourself a hell of a fishing partner. Some parts of some rivers had places where a female couldn't man-age, and they needed different equipment sometimes, because their muscle structure is different from men's. But they became good casters easier than men, and they became experts with flytying and flies, because of their inherent gentility."

Deren's wife, Catherine, is a nice-looking woman, who

was wearing slacks and a blouse and had her hair piled up in a bouffant hairdo the one time I saw her in the shop. She was as nice as pie to me then. Her perfume was unusual in that room filled with the smells of fly-tying cement, rubber, canvas, and True cigarette smoke. Another time, I saw her on the street, and she had just had some dental work done and she was really in pain and did not want to talk at all.

In *The Origins of Angling*, the author, John McDonald, says that angling existed in the ancient world, and that our knowledge of modern angling dates from 1496, when *A Treatyse of Fysshynge wyth an Angle*, by Dame Juliana Berners, was published in England. He says that hunting and falconry were the sports of medieval chivalry, that books on those sports had existed for centuries, that the publication of the *Treatyse* occurred at about the same time as the decline of chivalry, and that the *Treatyse* is addressed to all who are, in its words, "virtuous, gentle, and freeborn," rather than just to the nobility. He says that it cannot be definitely proved that Dame Juliana Berners wrote the book, as people say, or that she was a nun, as people also say. He says that people fished with tackle that was basically the same as that described in the *Treatyse* until the eighteenth and nineteenth centuries, when the invention of a better reel, of upstream fishing, and of the trout fly that floated rather than sank changed the sport tremendously. He says that over the centuries there has been much argument about trout-fly patterns, that the *Treatyse* presented twelve trout flies, for the different months of the year, as if they stood for immutable truths, that these twelve ruled for a hundred and seventy-five years, until Charles Cotton's *Instructions*

How to Angle for a Trout or Grayling in a Clear Stream introduced sixty-five new fly patterns, that in the eighteenth century Richard and Charles Bowlker entered the discussion with their *A Catalogue of Flies Seldom Found Useful to Fish With*, and that the dispute continues to the present. The idea is that some anglers like to use the flies that have always worked, while others like to experiment. McDonald says, "The trout fly is still subject to a constant pull between classicism and innovation. In recorded history, the score is now even: three dominantly classical centuries—the fifteenth, sixteenth, and eighteenth; and three innovating—the seventeenth, nineteenth, and twentieth."

So when Deren says, as he often does, "What in the hell is the point of using a famous fly that is some imported concoction from some Scottish salmon river which is probably the result of some guy having a couple of martinis a hundred and fifty years ago, which doesn't look a thing like any insect on any stream in this country, and which never looked like any insect in the British Isles, either, when you can pick a bug off a rock and copy it and catch a fish?" he speaks in the voice of his century.

Much of angling today is disappointing. Some of the best trout streams in the country are now privately owned, and it costs a lot of money per person for a day of fishing, and you have to get your reservations a long time in advance. The health advisory included in every copy of the fishing regulations for the state of Michigan says that because of the high PCB, PBB, and mercury content of fish from Lake Michigan, Lake Huron, and many of their tributary streams, no one should eat more than half a pound per week of fish caught in these waters, and pregnant women or women who one day expect to have children should not eat any at all. The acid rain that falls in the Catskill Mountains is bad for fish, so now fisheries biologists in New York State are trying to breed a strain of acid-resistant fish. In the absence of clean streams that are nearby and uncrowded and full of wild trout, the modern angler often concentrates on a particular aspect of his sport—one that does not require such a rare set of circumstances. Some people like to cast, and they become tournament casters; some people read about fishing all the time; some people write about it.

Deren concentrates on tackle, of course; he also concentrates on information. Information is vital to angling. The fact that anglers are always hungry for information is probably one of the reasons *The Compleat Angler* has gone through over three hundred editions since it first appeared. Anglers are always trying to find out how to fish, where to fish, when to fish, what to fish. They always want to know about new killer lures, new techniques, new hot spots nobody else knows. Nowadays, it is often easier to buy the most esoteric piece of equipment than it is to obtain a really great piece of information. An angling writer will tell about the tremendous fishing on some tremendous stream, and then add that he's not going to give the name or site of the stream, for fear that all his readers will go there and ruin it. Most angling information is subjective. A theory that one person puts into practice with confidence works fine for him but may be worse than useless to the person with no confidence in it—sort of like literature or medicine. Every angler knows one fishing secret that he thinks nobody else knows. One person will say he's just discovered the greatest fly or the greatest technique of all time, then another will come along and say it's the dumbest thing he's ever heard of, and so on. It is a cliché that fishermen are big liars, but some fishermen actually are. Sometimes the land of angling information is like that land in the riddle where half the inhabitants tell the truth all the time and the other half lie.

All day long, Deren hands out and receives angling information. People are eager to share with him the one thing they know. Sometimes he will throw cold water on them by giving them an answer that begins with his standard "That's one of the great misconceptions of fly-fishing." Sometimes (less often) he will tell them they are absolutely right. His agreement or disagreement is never less than vehement. A very large number of people, in his opinion, have no idea what they are talking about. He says, "You follow something long enough and you realize you know as much as—or *more than*—anyone else, and that opens up a door. Most of this knowledge is based on having the problem yourself and solving it. A guy can come in here and ask me a question and I'll know I can answer his Questions 1, 2, and 3. But it might be two years before the guy comes in and asks Question No. 2." And when Deren is right (as he was when he told me how to catch a trout on that April day) he's really right. In the world of angling information, he gives the impression of knowing everything, and it is this impression that's important. If the stream of people who flow through New York bring Deren sustenance, then it is the weedy tangle of angling information, of statement and contradiction and myth and old wives' tale and supposition and theory and actual fact growing out of five hundred years of angling, that provides him with cover.

I have never fished with Deren, but once (although I did not know it at the time) I fished near Deren. One year I fished in

Montana for two months—mostly in the Yellowstone River, near the town of Livingston. Deren goes out to Montana in the early fall just about every year, so when I got back to New York I went to see him. I asked him if he'd ever been to Livingston. "You're goddamn right I been to Livingston. I was hit by a truck in Livingston," he said. (He and his wife were in their camper, pulling into a gas station, when a kid in a pickup truck ran into them. Deren was not hurt, but his wife had to have her arm X-rayed. Nothing broken.) I asked him if he had ever fished at a place where I fished a lot, called the Sheep Mountain Fishing Access. "I remember smells, I remember the way things look, I remember sounds, but I don't remember names," he said. (I know this is true. Despite the fact that I have talked to him for many hours, and despite that fact that when I first introduced myself to him he said, "That's a good name for you," I doubt very much if Deren has any idea what my name is. But when I call him on the phone he always recognizes my voice right away.)

"Sheep Mountain is downstream from the bridge on the road that leads to White Sulphur Springs," I said. "The river breaks up into lots of channels there. There are a bunch of islands."

"Yeah, I know the place you're talking about. I've fished there. Not last time we were out. Last time we camped on the river upstream from there."

"Just this fall?"

"Yeah. We got to the Yellowstone on October 10."

October 10 was my last full day in Montana. I fished all day, very hard, because I had not caught the fish I had dreamed I would catch out there. The river had filled up with mud and little pieces of moss right after I arrived, in mid-August—a man in a fishing-tackle store told me that a whole cliff had washed away in a rainstorm, up in Yellowstone Park, near the river's source—and it stayed muddy for several weeks. Then, after it cleared, the weather became hot and the water level dropped, and my luck stayed bad. I threw nymphs, among them Deren's big stone flies, and grasshopper imitations and bee imitations and ants and dragonflies all over the river every day. I caught whitefish and unimpressive trout. (Just before I left, I told that same man in the tackle store the size of the largest trout I'd caught during my stay, and he winced and went "Oooh!"—as if I had shown him a nasty bruise on my forehead.) On my last day, I took a lunch, drove to the fishing access, fished my way several miles upstream, crossed a bridge, and worked my way more than several miles back downstream. When I noticed that it was getting dark, I was on the opposite side of the river from my car, and miles from the bridge. I started through the brush back to the bridge. The beavers who live along the river cut saplings with their teeth at a forty-five-degree angle. These chisel-pointed saplings are unpleasant to fall on. The fishing net dangling from my belt wanted to stop and make friends with every tree branch in Montana. Occasionally I would stop and swear for three or four minutes straight. At one of these swearing stops I happened to look across the river, and I saw my car where I had parked it, lit up in the headlights of a passing car. I calculated: there was my car, just across the big, dark, cold Yellowstone; it was many more miles of underbrush to the bridge, and miles from the bridge back to the car; the river was down from its usual level, and I had forded it not far from this spot a few days before; but then that was during the day, and now I couldn't even see the other bank unless a car drove by. I waded in. I wasn't wearing waders. It took a second for the water to come through my shoes. It was cold. My pants ballooned around my shins. The water came past my knees, past my thighs. Then it got *really* cold. I was trying to keep my shoulders parallel to the flow of the river. The water came to my armpits, and my feet were tiptoeing along the pebbles on the river bottom. I still couldn't see the bank before me, and when I glanced behind me I couldn't see that bank, either. I was going downstream fast. Then I realized that, gathered up tight and holding my arms out of the water, I had not been breathing. I took a deep breath, then another, and another. When I did, I saw all around me, under my chin in the dark water, the reflections of many stars. The water was not getting any deeper. I was talking to myself in reassuring tones. Finally, the water began to get shallower. Then it got even shallower. Then I was strolling in ankle-deep water on a little shoal about a quarter mile downstream from my car. I walked up onto the bank and sang a couple of bars from "We Will Rock You," by Queen. Then I raised my arms and kissed my biceps. I walked to my car and drove back to the house I was staying in and took an Olympia beer out of the refrigerator and drank it. The motto of Olympia beer is "It's the Water." That night, I had a physical memory of the river. It was a feeling of powerful current pushing against my left side so insistently that I had to keep overcoming the illusion that I was about to be washed out of bed.

"Did you fish that day, on the tenth? How did you do?" I asked.

"Oh, that first day we were on the Yellowstone I hardly even got out of the camper," Deren said. "I was pooped from driving, and I honestly did not think that conditions were at all favorable. The water was down, it was too bright. I did take one walk down to the river, for the benefit of these two guys who were following me. When I'm in Montana, guys follow me wherever I go, because they think I'll lead them to good fishing. I showed these two guys a piece of holding water where they might find some big trout, and then I went back to the camper. Later that evening, after dark, the guys came to my camper, banged on the door, woke me and Catherine up. They had this goddamn huge brown trout they'd caught, right where I told them. They were pretty happy about that."

"I didn't catch any big trout, but that same night I forded the river," I said.

Deren looked at me. "That's a big river," he said.

On the inside of the door to his shop Deren has posted what is probably his most famous maxim: "There don't have to be a thousand fish in a river; let me locate a good one and I'll get a thousand dreams out of him before I catch him—and, if I catch him, I'll turn him loose."

For Larry Madison, a wildlife photographer and magazine editor who often fished with Deren thirty years ago, a thousand dreams were hundreds more than his patience could stand: "Jim would get in a pool and just pound it all day. I'd say, 'Oh, Christ, you been in there for ten hours and you haven't had a hit. Let's go home.' Not him."

Fishing is worth any amount of effort and any amount of expense to people who love it, because in the end you get such a large number of dreams per fish. You can dream about a fish for years before the one moment when your fly is in the right place, when something is about to happen, when you hold your breath and time expands like a bubble until suddenly fish and fisherman feel each other's live weight. And for a long time afterward the memory of that moment gives you something you can rest your mind on at night, just before sleep.

·

(The last word I had from Deren came via my brother-in-law, John Hayes. A few months after this article appeared, in 1982, I moved to Montana. That December, John stopped by the Roost, and Deren asked why I hadn't been coming around. John said that I was now living in northwest Montana. Deren said, "Tell him, 'Don't drown.' " Jim Deren died, and the Angler's Roost closed, the following year.)

ON THE AUSABLE

On the West Branch of the Ausable, an Adirondack river three hundred miles north of Manhattan, the stone looks the same as the stone downstate, only wilder. Big rocks of the kind that people sun themselves on in Central Park spill down the bed of the river, which sometimes pools around them and sometimes rushes by, white and fast; granite boulders the light gray or rose-pink of building fronts sit in mid-current in skirts of eddies; smaller boulders on the stream edge make a chain of bathtub-sized pools filled by small waterfalls. Looking into some larger pools from above, you can see sharp-edged blocks of granite lying toppled on the bottom. Tea-colored water pours steadily over lips as smooth as subway stairs. Cliffs of granite climb from the river in small terraces of pine and alder. Crotches between streamside boulders collect bunches of driftwood, along with spiderwebs and pine straw and pieces of broken picnic cooler lids and wads of fishing line. The underwater rocks are so slick with gray-green algae that you have to grope along each one with your foot as you wade. Felt-soled boots are a must;

wading staffs, too. The smooth granite of the big boulders, cool in the morning, warm on a sunny afternoon, does not give you much to grab on to when the current starts to pull. In the fast sections, the sound of the main channels is so loud it overpowers the smaller noises of streamlets at the edge. Underneath the rushing is a deep, muffled grinding of the rocks in the bed. The sound is like a train passing under the street. I don't wade out in mid-current unless I really need to. At a place miles from any town I saw a boulder a ways out in the river with a strange marking. Slipping, sliding, turning sidewise against the current, nearly falling, I waded to it. The mark was a borehole, a hole drilled for blasting at a quarry or a construction site. There is an old quarry near the river someplace far upstream. I climbed onto the boulder, noticed a likely place I couldn't have reached before, braced my knee in the borehole, cast. My dry fly, an Ausable Wulff, had less than a second to sit on some slack water before the current would snatch it. A rainbow trout shot to the surface, took the fly, dived.

In 1950, the angling writer Ray Bergman, in his book *Trout*, described the West Branch of the Ausable:

A river rife with fishing legends, the home of numerous trout; a stream wildly fascinating, capable of giving you both a grand time and a miserable one; a stream possessing a Dr. Jekyll and Mr. Hyde temperament and a character strong enough to spread its fame from one corner of our country to the other. The Ausable commands your respect. It tests your skill and ingenuity. It is not a stream that will appeal to the timid, the weak, or the old. You like it best before you reach the age of forty. After that you wish you had youthful energy so that you could enjoy it as you did before the years of striving for existence had sapped your strength and made you a bit fearful of slippery rocks and powerful currents.

He does not mention the blackflies. When I stepped from my car late one morning in June, the sunny forest of conifers and hardwoods directed them at me like a ray. I got back in the car immediately and drove to Au Sable Forks and bought some Cutter insect repellent in a solid tube. At the elementary school there, it was recess; kids stood around on the playground twitching and swatting. I rolled the repellent over all exposed skin, stinging that morning's razor cuts. On the river, when I began to sweat—chest waders can be suffocating—drops flavored with repellent got into my mouth and made my lips tingle. The flies orbited me at several quantum levels, chewed my forearms through my shirtsleeve vents, made inroads under my collar, took long excursions between T-shirt and skin. I continued upstream, swatting and casting, slithering over rocks, splashing, stomping down brush. I didn't see a single fish. Nothing touched my dry fly, I got no strikes on my nymph. It began to rain lightly, then to pour. I decided to go back to the car. I left the river and climbed a steep cliff and got lost. I found an old logging road, followed it to a gravel road. By a hard-to-explain theory, I reasoned that if I just kept turning left at every intersection I would end up at the car. The theory turned out to be correct; however, the counterclockwise loop I described in the process covered perhaps five miles. I went up and down hills, on paved roads and unpaved. Rain fell so hard it made a loud noise on my hat. Even the money in my wallet got wet.

This particular trip, I was going nuts because I had not

caught a fish in a while. In fact, I had fished two days on the river the month before without catching anything at all. People say, "Well, it's nice just to get out." But when you're not catching anything, a heron flies by with wings creaking like a wooden pump handle, and a kingfisher ratchets over the water, and a beaver with its hair slicked back swims at you and spots you and pounds the water with its tail as it dives, and a robin flies back and forth across the river with something in its bill on each return trip, and a cedar waxwing stops in midair to snatch an insect, and a white gull flies along the river course and disappears around a bend, and two woodcocks go up, one after the other, from a patch of alders, and bluets and violets and purple trilliums and swamp buttercups bloom along the bank, and it all seems vaguely to make fun of you. I'm not really there until I catch a fish. I reached the car, finally, and took off my stuff and drove, soaking wet, to another place on the river without stopping to eat.

The West Branch of the Ausable contains lots of different kinds of water, from rapids to dammed-up narrow lake to waterfall flume to deep pool to slow, semi-marshy meadow stream. Actually, that's almost in reverse order. The river's upper reaches, near the town of Lake Placid, flow over mud-and-sand bottom through a level valley, sometimes past an expanse of potato fields. I had seen big fish rising on that upstream section the year before. It is thirty or more river miles from Au Sable Forks, about twenty by car. I parked behind several other cars at a one-lane bridge over the river. Fly fishermen were standing in the water upstream and down. I walked a long way upstream and emerged from the brush and saw another fisherman. I continued until I couldn't see anyone. I was hoping to coincide with a hatch of the big mayfly called the green drake. A big hatch or spinnerfall of green drakes can make the river percolate with feeding trout.

As soon as I stepped into the river, a mayfly disengaged itself from the surface film and flew waveringly by me. I snatched it from the air, saw that it was a green drake, and ate it. Mayflies taste a little like grass stems, and have a similar crunch. Once, I was fishing the Sturgeon River, in Michigan, with my friend Don when drakes began to hatch, and the trout fed so eagerly, chasing insects five feet across the surface and coming clear out of the water and slapping logs with their tails and gulping and splashing, that we got hungry, too. We began to grab insects from the water and the air. They were like hors d'oeuvres, little winged shrimp. They left a bitter aftertaste and a dryness, but no other ill effects, and they do fill you up.

This time I saw no drakes after that first one. The blackflies were as bad here as downstream. On my way I had passed a man fishing in beekeepers' netting. I fished listlessly and hopelessly. Two guys came by spin-fishing from a canoe and politely dragged it through a shallow channel rather than disturb the deep channel where I was. They asked if I was having any luck (that's what you ask, I've found, in the East; out West, the query is "Doin' any good?"), and I said no, and they said they'd just started. Hours later, I still hadn't caught anything. At least the wading here was easier than in the rapids. I ambled with the current, waist deep, half buoyant, bouncing along like someone walking on the moon. I got out and went through brush when I neared other fishermen. The river began to take on that sort of metallic color of a river with no fish in it. I kept casting out of nerve reflex and changing flies faithlessly. The guys in the canoe paddled by again; they had been downstream and were now just cruising around. At my question, the guy in the stern reached down, fumbled for a moment, and, with both hands, lifted one of the biggest rainbow trout I had ever seen. It was two feet long, its belly sagged, its silver sides had just begun to fade in patches of discoloration.

This revived my concentration wonderfully. I tied on a weighted fly meant to imitate a crayfish—I had noticed bleached shells of crayfish claws in mud along the bank—and flailed it all over the river. It was the size of a hood ornament and caused me to flinch and duck as it whistled past. I lost it on a birch log. I tied on another fly and kept flailing. Rain began to fall again, and lightning flashed. As I approached the pool under the one-lane bridge, the guy who was fishing there left. I moved up to and past where he had been. Close to the bridge I saw a fish hit the surface—the first rise I had seen all day. I tied on a White Wulff—a fly that resembles the green drake. I cast, watched the fly float among raindrop splashes. A fish rose, and I set the hook. I knew from the fight that this would be a decent-sized fish. I maneuvered him alongside and scooped him up in my net.

I am tempted to lie about how big he was, because it sort of embarrasses me to have been so pleased with a sleek, plump brown trout of no more than twelve inches. But there it is: I felt fine. Calm, justified, highly skilled, even a little dangerous. I released the trout and stepped from the river into the Adirondack scenery, to which I now belonged. I walked to my car. Up ahead, I saw the ski-jump towers used in the 1980 Lake Placid Winter Olympics. One tower is ninety meters high and the other is seventy. Lights to warn airplanes blink on top of the taller one. The rest of the structures were dark against the dim gray sky. John Brown, the abolitionist, is buried a few hundred yards on the other side of the towers. He had a farm here in the 1850s, when he helped to build a community of free blacks, called Timbucto. A New York abolitionist gave the colonists the land, but John Brown paid for his own farm. After he was hanged for the raid on Harpers Ferry, his wife brought him back here by train, boat, and wagon. Eleven of his sons and followers lie in the small cemetery with him. John Brown loved this place, and pointed out the beauty of the scenery to his children. The mountains—Whiteface, Marcy, and others—reminded him of the fortresses in the Alleghenies he had planned as refuges for the slaves he would free. He lies next to a cabin-sized outcrop of granite in his former front yard.

Another morning, my wife and daughter dropped me off at the river near the ski jumps. They were going to Santa's Workshop, a little-kid amusement park in Wilmington, and would return in the evening. The day was hot and still. Trout were rising all up and down the river, feeding on tiny mayflies called tricos. These insects are the size of half a little-fingernail paring, or smaller, and the artificials that imitate them require tiny hooks with tiny eyes attached to wispy, hair-fine leaders. Working in such dimensions is right at the limit of my patience and dexterity. Many anglers ignore the trico hatches altogether. I found a fly that looked good in my box of tiny ones, and tied it to an 8X leader. Casting something so light and so hard to see is an activity bordering on mime. Finally, I put the fly more or less where I wanted it, and spotted it after it landed, thanks to its white wings. Fish rose all around it but ignored it. I switched to another fly—same result. I tied on tiny fly after tiny fly. The fish continued to rise eagerly. My flies floated unscathed through rising fish like plucky couriers through bomb explosions in a war movie.

I worked my way far downstream and stopped at a gravel beach for lunch. A water snake zigzagged fast across the surface, in what looked like a shoelacing race. A hummingbird approached a honeysuckle bush in a series of right-angle lines, emerging from each blossom with a small, businesslike chirp. Suddenly I decided I should be fishing someplace far from where I was. I took off downstream, going overland through the brush so as not to disturb the water. There had been plenty of rain, and the bottomland was especially jungly. My too-small waders caused me to walk penguin-style—a style that inhibited leaps and vaults. I suffered several pratfalls. I thrashed through deep brush for forty minutes or more. At one point, a dead tree had fallen onto the dense willows and alders, providing a kind of elevated highway. I walked on the tree until a rotten part of it gave and dumped me into the understory. More plunging and thrashing. I emerged onto a red-muck section of riverbank and breathed deep and looked at my watch. It was gone.

The watch had been my father's, a gift from my mother inscribed with a motto and the date of their marriage. She gave it to me after he died. My mind swerved toward panic, imagining the sad-sack story I would tell my wife, and how sorry she and my sisters would be for me. I looked back at the brush I'd been in for half a mile. No way, man. Then I took off my waders—I had ripped out the crotch in the brush—and put my wading shoes back on. The watch must be somewhere. It was shiny metal. I had time before dark. Once I got back in the brush, it all looked the same, and I could not find where I'd been. I found boggy places with no footprints in them. I kept going, tacking back and forth. Off to the left, through the green gloom, I recognized the fallen tree I'd walked on. I climbed on it again, traced my path to the place I'd fallen. Suddenly, among the nondescript broken gray branches below, I saw the brown of the leather watchband, and there it was, there the watch was! I held it in my right hand and raised it in the air and hoorahed.

(1993)

ON URBAN SHORES

My friend Tim and I used to hit golf balls into the water from the shoreline of lower Manhattan. Tim ordered the balls by the gross, used, from a golfing magazine; they had scuffs, smiles, spray-painted dots, and legends like "Tri-County Challenge—'80" and "Lost by Dan Trivino" and "Molub-Alloy The Metallic Lubricant" and "Maintenance Supply Co. Huntersville N.C." We told ourselves we were working on our drives. All we needed was a place open to the water; usually, we could find cracks in the asphalt or concrete big enough to fit a tee. We picked our targets. Once, I tried to land a ball on a mattress going out with the tide on the East River. I didn't succeed, but it would have been cool if I had. Once, I bounced a flat, hard drive off the stone base of the nearer tower of the Manhattan Bridge. A following shot struck the inside of an immense, upreaching I-beam, ricocheted to the opposite inside, then sped diagonally down into the water. Tim hit a beauty across a dredged inlet by a construction site at Battery Park City, the ball socking into a distant pile of sand and burying itself in a small landslide. One that he aimed at a passing container ship fell just short of the hull with a white exclamation point of a splash. My best shot came from a pier on the Lower East Side one winter morning with five inches of snow on the ground. Placing the ball on snow had a psychological effect on me, and I hit perfect drive after perfect drive. A cargo ship came along, well out in the channel. I took careful aim, kept my head down, and stroked one of those unstoppable balls that seem to rise like music, octave by octave—would it hit that glass housing near the bow? would they call the Coast Guard?—as the ship moved but not fast enough: ship and ball intersected, and a puff of snow came from a metal hatch cover amidships. Half a second later we heard the impact's muffled clang. The name of the vessel was the *John B. Carroll.*

Just after dawn one day, we were hitting off an abandoned pier by Rutgers Slip, upstream from the Manhattan Bridge, when a little guy who had been sitting there on a folding metal chair came over and began to talk to us. Pointing to the water, he said, "See that? Those're anchovies. Like you put on pizza." Until then, I had never looked closely at the water of the East River—assuming the worst about it, I suppose—but now I observed that it was indeed full of silver-sided baitfish swirling and boiling like noodles in soup. The school was thick down as deep as you could see. The guy continued to talk about anchovies and other subjects as we continued to hit. He had a hand line with what looked like a piece of lime-green surgical tubing for a lure. When he left, he picked up from among some broken pallets a big striped bass he had caught. We had not noticed the fish before. He carried it off— to sell in Chinatown, he said—by a scrap of plastic packing rope strung through its mouth and gills.

Soon after that, we saw in *The New York Times* that the

International Maritime Organization had issued a prohibition against ocean dumping of non-biodegradable plastics—a category that would include golf balls. To protect sea life, the ruling applied to all oceangoing vessels and to cruise ships' profitable practice of selling golf balls for passengers to hit. We had suspected that what we were doing qualified as minor vandalism; now, thanks to the I.M.O., we were sure. So we stopped (there is now a net-enclosed driving range on one of the Hudson River piers we used to use), and I began to think more about the guy with the striped bass. I had read about stripers—the game fish that can grow to fifty or sixty pounds or more, the trophy species sought by thousands of oilskin-clad surf anglers, the voracious schooling fish that sometimes chase mullet and menhaden and tinker mackerel up onto the beach, the anadromous swimmer that lives most of its life in the ocean and spawns locally in the Hudson River—but I had never fished for them.

I began to scout up and down the shoreline in Manhattan on bright fall afternoons. At a rotted wooden pipe that had the appearance of a large barrel extending into the East River at Twentieth Street, I saw alewives nosing against moss-covered pilings. More bait appeared in the semi-clear water in sudden relief against the dark background of a drowned car seat. In fact, from Twenty-third Street all the way down to the tip of Corlears Hook, just south of Grand Street, the East River depths glinted with shifting schools of bait. All the books say that where there's bait there are stripers. I bought a nine-foot surf-casting rod and a spinning reel with twenty-pound-test line. I bought one-ounce white leadhead jigs with tails of white bucktail hair, and other lures. Stripers are known to move at dawn, to feed by first light. I woke up at four one morning and took the subway to Manhattan from my apartment, in Brooklyn—the first time I had ever approached a fish by going under it. "Striped bass," the token-booth clerk said when he saw my fishing rod. I rode with transit workers in orange-mesh vests carrying sacks of tokens and accompanied by armed guards, got off at the East Broadway stop, and walked down to the East River in the late night of Chinatown. A starling's raspy cry startled me. Police cars idled; clouds of steam from a steam tunnel crossed the street.

At the southern end of Corlears Hook Park is a graffiti-covered brick structure about the size of a shed, which extends into the river. The structure has no windows—only metal vents on two sides. Maybe it is part of an airshaft for an underwater tunnel. Warm air comes from the vents sometimes, and people who fish here call the structure the Heat House. A good cast from the Heat House's concrete apron can reach a tidal rip that forms on water ebbing around this corner of Manhattan Island. I set up my rod and tied on a lure by the light of a streetlight and went through a break in a chain-link fence. A man was sleeping on the concrete behind the Heat House, however, in the warm air from the vents. He had one shoe on, the other beneath his head. I moved to the walkway along the river upstream and began to fish there. The bottom of the river must be a cluttered spot—I hung up lure after lure. At first light, gulls began to fly by. I heard the rattle of shopping-cart wheels as a bottle-and-can-collecting guy appeared. The man behind the Heat House woke up and left, and I took his place. I was casting the bucktail jig about fifty yards to the tide rip, retrieving with short, quick pulls. Truck traffic on the Manhattan Bridge had slowed to a standstill, and on the bridge's lower level the bright beads of the D-train windows slid back and forth. Occasional passing barges sent wakes sloshing along the shore. The first jogger went by, singing tonelessly with his Walkman. At almost the moment of sunrise, about four minutes past seven, I felt a strong resistance on my line. I thought at first that I was hung up again. Then the resistance began to move. I pumped and reeled, gaining line. I still wasn't sure what I would pull out of there—an infant car seat, say, would have been only a mild surprise. But then the resistance was pulling, jerking. In the murky water I saw a flash of white, then stripes—a striper! It was about two feet long, and bent my rod double as I tried to hoist it out. Then there it was, slapping around on the concrete.

Striped bass are in many respects the perfect New York fish. They go well with the look of downtown. They are, for starters, pinstriped; the lines along their sides are black fading to light cobalt blue at the edges. The dime-sized silver scales look newly minted, and there is an urban glint to the eye and a mobility to the wide predator jaw. If they could talk, they would talk fast. Although really big stripers take on a no-neck, thuggish, rectangular look, ones this size are classically proportioned—fish a child would draw. I unhooked mine and picked it up with both hands. All muscle, it writhed; a sharp spine of the dorsal fin went into my hand, and—thump, bump—the fish was back in the water and gone. A woman jogger doing leg-stretching exercises on the fence looked at me unsmiling, as if I were a fish abuser. Generally, when I fish I am in the woods, standing in weeds or mud or sand. Hauling a fish into the city like this made both city and fish more vivid—as if a striped bass had suddenly arrived flopping on my desk. A few casts later, I hooked another. It was about the same size but fought harder, and I had more trouble getting the hook out. Scales scraped off on the concrete as I held the fish down. I was too high up to reach the water and so could not rinse the slime from my hands. I let the fish go; here a striper must be thirty-six inches long before you can keep it. (Also, because of the danger of contamination from PCBs and other chemicals, the State Department of Health recommends that people eat little or no fish caught in New York Harbor.) I broke down my rod and walked back to the subway and got home in time to take my daughter to school.

I wanted to catch more and bigger stripers. I got striper fever. I read outdoor columns about stripers in newspapers and picked up angling newsletters in tackle shops and called recorded fishing tapes at a dollar forty-five a minute and talked to closemouthed striper anglers. In a tackle store in Bay Ridge, several striper anglers trading stories dropped their voices and leaned toward one another as I approached. Striper anglers have big, gill-like necks, wear clothing in layers, and yawn ostentatiously in daylight. They are famous for their divorce rate; the striper is a night creature, and its pursuers must be, too. I fished for stripers all this fall. Mostly, I went to Sandy Hook, the expanse of barrier beach bent like a crooked arm from the Jersey shore at the southern approach to New York Harbor. Sandy Hook is visible from Brooklyn, and from Sandy Hook you can see the Verrazano Narrows Bridge, the lower Manhattan skyline, and the sunrise on the windows of apartment buildings in Brighton Beach. People have caught many big stripers at Sandy Hook; it is among the prime striper-fishing grounds on the East Coast.

I knew nothing about fishing in surf. At first it feels funny to park in a beach parking lot (Sandy Hook's beaches are all part of a national recreation area), put on chest waders, rig up, walk to an ocean stretching thousands of miles to Spain, and cast. My first day, I fished along the beach for several miles, using a swimming plug bigger than many trout I've been happy to catch. Casting it was hard work. I didn't know for sure how far into the ocean I should wade. A big wave knocked me down onto one arm. I climbed back on the beach and saw a sign in the distance. I thought perhaps it warned of dangerous surf. I walked over to it. It said:

ATTENTION.
BEYOND THIS POINT
YOU MAY ENCOUNTER
NUDE SUNBATHERS

The wind was blowing hard, lifting sand in smoky wraiths and rattling it against pieces of plastic trash. A half-buried strip of photographic film flapped rapidly with an industrial sound; it had dug a sharp-edged trench beside itself. The temperature was about fifty degrees—not nude-sunbathing weather. As I continued, however, I passed a trim bronze naked guy accompanying a clothed female, then a trio of old guys strolling along in hats, sweatshirts, dark glasses, sneakers, knee socks, and no pants. One guy said hello. I said hello back.

Mostly, I fished in the hours just before and after dawn. Sandy Hook, maybe twelve air miles from my apartment, is about an hour and a quarter away by car. I drove across Staten Island and through Jersey in light traffic, listening to radio programs with few commercials, sometimes following into a toll booth the four-wheel-drive vehicle of another striper angler. The millions in their beds on a full-moon night in October may not know that the beaches nearby are lined with hundreds of striper anglers, mostly men but some women, looking seaward as if awaiting an invasion. Darkness makes them more solitary. Anglers rig up by their cars' overhead lights and walk to the beach thirty feet apart in silence. I passed many anglers in the dark but never exchanged a word. When you can't really see the ocean, you hear it and smell it more. On clear mornings, dawn came up full and sudden, like houselights in a theater, and the sun followed along behind. Venus was bright on the horizon to the northeast at 5 a.m. On cloudy mornings, dawn was dull, with occasional surprises: a red sun would pop up on the horizon, chin itself on a low ceiling of gray, and disappear for good; or, though the horizon stayed dark, silvery light would glisten on the water, and from a break in the clouds, celestially high, beams from the sunrise would spill down.

Sometimes the waves were like high hedges. Sometimes the sea just sat there and swayed; then, all of a sudden, a breaker would *whump* and the foam would be up under my arms. I cast and reeled, cast and reeled. A moment came when I could see my lure in the air as I cast, and a later moment when I could make out its succinct splash. The birds woke. If the tide was going out, gulls by the thousand occupied the exposed sand. A gull picked up a clam, dropped it to break the shell, failed, and kept on trying. Flocks of little gray-and-white shorebirds—sanderlings?—stayed right at the waves' edges. Long combers ran the birds back up the beach like the flat of a hand pushing crumbs. As waves rolled to the shore, they made white broken shells on the bottom hop up into them with a sort of vacuum-cleaner effect. Pieces of shells bounced from the waves' tops. I sometimes hooked a shell or a piece of clam but (at first) no fish of any kind. After full daylight, the anglers began to give up and came walking back to their cars. They wore yellow slickers, red-and-black-checked hunting caps, camouflage coveralls, Penn State sweatshirts. At the ends of their lines dangled swimming plugs, popping plugs, rigged eels, sandworms, bloodworms, gobs of clams the size of baseballs. Some guys said the fish weren't here yet, or the mullet hadn't arrived to draw them, or the water was too murky or still too warm.

One morning I brought peanut-butter-and-jelly sandwiches and bottled water, and stayed. By eight-thirty, along the whole expanse of beach I could see only one other angler. As I watched, his rod bent. I walked toward him and saw him land a big fish and let it go. When I got near, I began to cast. I had switched to the same leadhead jig that had worked in the East River; most of the white paint had been scraped off it by now. At once, I felt a hard, unmistakable hit, and the line went tight. Briefly, the fish took line, and, briefly, I hoped it would be big. The line was going right into the near-vertical side of a wave; at the base of a following wave I saw a swirl from the tail. I backed up the beach and slid the fish out of the foam and into a rivulet the ebbing tide had cut in the sand. It was a striper, good-sized but still not legal, hooked at the hinge of the jaw. I held it up and the other angler yelled, "Way to go!" I set it back in the surf.

At a tackle store in nearby Atlantic Highlands, amid sand spikes to hold rods on the beach, lead-loaded priests for clubbing fish, spiked cleats for climbing on jetties, bottles of fish scent to spray on lures, basins of wildly wriggling eels, and snapshots of stripers bigger than a six-year-old child, I talked to a veteran striper angler named Frank. He worked there and had caught some of the fish in the pictures. He gave me a number of tips, among them the fact that stripers love bad weather—the worse the weather, the more the stripers like it. As a result, one afternoon I fished in a storm that descended from the north, covering the city and its lights like a fire blanket. I had to adjust my hat to the tightest fit, and when the rain hit my eyes it hurt. Wind blew spray from the wave crests like dust behind a car, and it rolled pieces of foam along the sand, where they dwindled in a blink. Whitish-brown foam covered the sea farther out than I could cast. Near some sunken rocks, I lost a lure, and accidentally put my next cast in the same spot. Reeling in fast to stay off the bottom, I felt a hard tug. The line started moving up the beach, I went with it, and the next thing I knew I had a striper on the sand at my feet. I hardly looked at it, in all the rain and spray: it was like something blown in by the storm, like a fish left in somebody's pants after a dousing in a cartoon. And, unfortunately, it was another "short," as the striper anglers call them. The bells of a buoy clanged and clanged. On the dim horizon, in the Ambrose Channel, a three-masted sailing ship in silhouette slowly headed for New York.

The striped bass never did show up in any numbers in the surf at Sandy Hook this fall, as near as I can tell. Striper anglers stood in the parking lots with their waders folded down around their middles and groused. Guys trudging back from the surf through the beach-plum bushes had similar expressions of frustration. A few talked about last year, or another year, and how the stripers were chasing bunkers in the wash at their feet, how the bluefish ate until the bait was coming out of their mouths, how some mornings every guy came home with a fish. This year, striper fishing was said to be good in the surf at Montauk, and in Staten Island Bay, and at Cape May, farther south in Jersey. But not, for some reason, here.

Striper season on the coast of New Jersey remains open all winter. The wind was blowing trash cans around on my street the last time I went out. On the Verrazano Bridge at 4 a.m., the car felt like a plane flying in turbulence. Street signs were shaking back and forth and flashing their reflections. As soon as I turned onto the road that runs along Sandy Hook, salt spray began to streak the windshield. I drove slowly down to Parking Area F, and as I got close, my headlights picked out the waves lurching from the dark like shrouded beings in a horror movie. They were mobbing the beach: there was no beach—just waves breaking so fast as to have no rhythm at all. The wind was trying to shout them down. I walked to take a closer look, and a speedy long surge chased me back. I decided I wanted to be in the car. As I backed out, a comber broke over the sand barrier and came down into the parking lot. I turned up the car heater and headed for home. People say the stripers will return again in May.

(1994)

FISHING WITHOUT DAD

My father did not fish. Unlike many non-anglers, he never even hefted a rod or tried a cast just to see what it was like. I never saw him with a piece of fishing equipment in his hand. He sometimes gave me advice about other sports; he was a research scientist and self-taught mathematician who liked to look for unexpected solutions to problems. For a while he entertained a theory that the next world record in the sprints might be made by a man trained to run on all fours, and once or twice he had me try to run on all fours on the front lawn. But on the subject of fishing he was silent. It just made no sense to him at all. The closest we ever came to fishing together was when I was ten or twelve and would fish from the pier by my grandmother's cottage on Lake Erie, while he occasionally sat and watched with the benign incomprehension you give to a dog worrying a leather toy on the rug. And if I ever caught something, he would croon, in pitying tones, "Ohhhh—let it go."

We lived in a small Ohio town that began to turn into a suburb upon our arrival. When I was sixteen, I fished one summer evening in a man-made pond in a housing development near town. I cast a willow-leaf spinner—an Abu-Reflex Shyster, with yellow bucktail hair and a yellow body with black spots—into a patch of water so weedy I could never have retrieved the lure if a largemouth hadn't hit the moment it landed. I reeled in, along with a bushel of weeds, the biggest bass I had ever seen. I could have fit a fist and a half in its open mouth. I showed it off around town and then brought it home on my stringer. Dad said, "Ohhhh no . . . is it too late to put him back?" When I told where I'd caught him, Dad said that that pond had been dug about the time we moved to town, and that the fish had probably been planted then and had probably lived in town as long as we had. Soon I felt as if I had hooked and killed one of my elementary school classmates. Guiltily, I cleaned the fish in the back yard. In the stomach I found a good-sized duckling—a brown blob with two perfectly preserved, delicate, orange webbed feet.

As long as no fish were actually caught, Dad tolerated fishing, but hunting he disliked and opposed under any circumstances. My parents were not too crazy about even toy guns; real guns were out of the question. I was not allowed them, or a BB gun, or a bow and arrow. The only arm I carried was a slingshot—the brand name was Wham-O and I owned a succession of wooden Wham-Os. I learned that you have to get pretty close to something pretty small to do it much damage with a slingshot. My hunting success was limited mostly to frogs. To compensate, I subscribed to outdoor magazines and read them closely. Disappointingly, they never had stories about people in my situation; on the contrary, they always seemed to have stories about a boy's first hunt with his dad, or about a boy at last catching a bigger fish than his dad's, or about a dad and a boy going to fish the old fishing hole one last time before the dad or the boy went off to war. These stories increased the regret with which I often regarded my dad, a mirror of his own regret that I had little interest in science or in helping him fix the car.

He loved to travel, and picked remote destinations—the more remote the better. Towing a camper trailer, our family drove all over the western United States and Canada for three weeks or more every summer, camping out. By coincidence, this took me right by some of the great trout rivers I had read about in the magazines. I sat in the back of the station wagon looking out the side windows at each river we passed. In Yellowstone Park I became kind of frantic as we drove over or along the Firehole, the Madison, the Yellowstone. Finally Dad said, "Oh hell, why don't we just stop and let the kid fish?" I was slightly taken aback—he did not often swear, he had never before referred to me as "the kid," and I had never thought of myself as a kid in the first place. I thought I was like him, only younger and smaller.

And of course, then, I didn't catch a thing. Uninformed reading had given me wacky ideas about trout fishing. I was using a spinning rod, a clear-plastic casting bubble, and a large Woolly Worm. It may be possible to catch a fish with such a rig, but I never did, not so much as a chub. None of the fishing played out as I had fantasized. At Fishing Bridge over the Yellowstone I saw a boy reel in a cutthroat trout and stab it with a sheath knife while drinking from a can of grape soda. I caught nothing at all in the great trout rivers of the West. Trout took on a mythical quality, like the snow leopard. Once, in the Bow River in Banff National Park in Canada, I was casting a red-and-white poplar-blade spinner in a tea-colored pool when suddenly, as the spinner approached through the underwater scenery, a big, swift, intent trout followed. I became unhinged and jerked the lure; the fish dematerialized; and I had to sit down against a tree. I then cast in the pool about a thousand more times, without result. Finally, I got the inspiration of removing the large Lake Erie sinkers I had been using on my worm rig and instead cast an unweighted nightcrawler hooked just once in the middle. The worm unfurled and drifted down in the currents like a silk scarf in a draft, and a rainbow trout instantly appeared and inhaled it. I yelled in triumph and Dad came running, expecting disaster. I showed him the fish and had him photograph me with it. In the photo, taken from a distance away, you can barely make out a fish not bigger than my hand.

Catch-and-release angling became popular just in time, as far as I was concerned. I had started fly-fishing in my teens, mainly because I thought a fly rod and reel looked so cool. I used to draw fly rods on my school notebooks the way other kids drew cars or fighter planes. But at first I caught even less fly-fishing than I had with my spinning rod. In Ohio I caught bluegills and bass in farm ponds, and on a family trip to Alaska I caught a lot of grayling; but still no trout. I had excuses—lack of skill and instruction and opportunity, loss of focus caused by late adolescence and the sixties. The truth is, I didn't catch a trout on a fly until I was twenty-five. A friend in Massachusetts took me to fish a brook with a series of beaver ponds, and I cast a Mickey Finn with an eye of real jungle-cock feather into a pool by the bridge where we had parked, and I felt a small strike, and I cast again and hooked an eight-inch brookie, and I went nuts but somehow landed the fish with my line draped and tangled among the bushes like popcorn ropes at Christmas. In following years I caught more trout, and bigger ones. It was actually a slight disappointment to learn that trout could indeed be caught just like any other fish. The more and bigger the fish, the louder the voice of my father in my head, and the more guilt I had to ignore. It was a great relief that as I became a more competent fisherman, fly-fishing opinion shifted in favor of letting the fish go.

My father died some years ago. If I had fished with him, I would now miss him on the stream; but, as I never did, he is still with me as much as ever. I often fish with friends, but I grew up fishing alone, and I still like to fish alone. When I do, the sense of my father as present in his absence is especially strong. If I get skunked, I reflect on the satisfaction he would feel that I had not injured anything today; and if I catch a fish, I sometimes see it through his pitying eyes. I have heard of a malady that sometimes comes over hunters when they kill a deer. I don't recall ever reading about a similar condition in fishing, but I get it—a sort of lunker fever, an odd emotional state that sometimes sweeps through me after I catch a big fish. I hold the fish in the shallows and move it gently to revive it and I talk to it and I get dizzy with the sensation of being in a moment that neither of us will forget. I tell the fish that I didn't mean to shake up its day and that I hope it will be all right and that it's a wonderful fish and that I hope it will never get caught again. And I feel scarily close to the fish's complex life that went on before and that will go on after, and close to my anxious, uncomprehending father, wherever he may be. When the fish and I are both more even-keeled, I take my hands away from its cold, nerved sides. Seconds pass; we realize we are no longer attached. I hear my father's "Ohhhh—let it go" as the fish swims away.

(1995)

BIG FISH, LITTLE FISH

Most angling stories involve big fish. For a fish to be literary, it must be immense, moss-backed, storied; for it to attain the level of the classics, it had better be a whale. But in fact, mostly that's not what we catch. Especially when first learning the sport, we catch little ones, and we continue to catch them even when we gain more skill and know how to find and fish for big ones. In the retelling, the little ones are enlarged, or passed over as if mildly shameful. There's just something not flattering about the contrast between overequipped us and a trophy that would fit with five others in a King Oscar of Norway Sardines can. You rarely read a story in which the author catches a fish of five inches—it's as if a fisherman's numbers don't go much below twelve. A recent euphemism is "fish of about a pound." When I hear of a slow day on the river where the angler is catching fish of about a pound, my mind corrects that estimate to "nine inches, tops."

I've told my personal big-fish stories so often to myself and others that now I may remember the stories better than the events they describe. The little fish I've caught remain un-glazed by myth, and if I do happen to remember them, they are perhaps in some ways more real than the big ones in my mind. Once, on the Yellowstone River, a pocket-sized rainbow trout startled me by coming clear out of a patch of riffle water to take a dry fly before it landed, when it was still about a foot in the air. Little rainbows are more vivid in color; this had a line like a streak of lipstick on its side. In a rivulet next to a campsite in northern Michigan, a friend and I heard small splashes one night as we sat around the fire. When we investi-gated with a flashlight, we saw a spring peeper frog swimming on the surface with one leg gone and fingerling brown trout slashing at him from below. Near the campsite ran the Pigeon River, a brushy stream full of browns. During a hendrickson hatch, I waded with great care toward a little sipping rise in a place almost impossible to cast to under tag-alder branches— just the sort of place you'd find an eighteen-inch fish. I hung up a fly or two, and broke them off rather than disturb the water. Finally, miraculously, I laid the fly in the exact spot; a four-inch brown hit so hard that his impetus carried him well up into the alder branches, where he remained, flipping and flapping and complicatedly entangling the line. Once in a river in Siberia reputed to hold *farel*, a troutlike game fish, I found instead millions of no-name silvery fish about the size of laun-dry marking pens. They were too small to net, but would take a fly; I caught fifteen or more, and a Russian friend wrapped each one whole in wet pages from her sketchbook and baked them, paper and all, in the campfire coals. We took them out and unwrapped them and ate them steaming hot, with river-temperature Chinese beer.

Little fish make my mouth water, like the mouths of the hungry cave-guys in the movie *Quest for Fire* when they see a herd of antelope across the plain. A seine net full of smelt looks delicious, almost as good as a dozen golden deep-fried smelt with lemon wedges on a plate. In Ohio we used to eat little fish by the mess—as in, a mess of bluegill or a mess of perch. My cousin and I used to catch white bass by the dozens in Lake Erie in the Painesville harbor, right by the docks of the Diamond Shamrock Chemical Company, and then take them back to his house for fish fries, which no doubt left certain trace elements that we carry with us to this day. Once, I was fishing for shad in the Delaware River with a friend and somehow snagged a minnow only slightly bigger than the fly itself. I showed it to my friend, examined it, and popped it in my mouth. His face did that special deep wince people do when they watch you eat something gross. But the taste wasn't bad—sushi, basically, only grittier.

When I went to Florida on a family vacation as a boy, I was disappointed to find that no tackle shop carried hooks small enough for the quarry I had in mind. Like everyone else I went out on the bottom-fishing boats in the deep water over the wrecks and the reefs. I cranked up a cobia longer than my leg, and a man from Cleveland in a scissorbill cap caught a shark which the captain finally had to shoot with a handgun. On later trips I remembered to bring small hooks and a spinning rod light enough to cast morsels of shrimp with no sinkers. In the quiet shade beneath the new overpass at the Key West charter-boat basin I fished for triggerfish, Frisbee-shaped fish with sharp dorsal spines and pursed, tiny mouths. They fought hard, turning sideways to the line and soaring among the pieces of rock and the mossy bases of the pilings. From the boardwalks of docks and next to highway bridges I fished for mangrove snappers, grunts, porgies, and unidentified fish with colors luminous as an expansion team's. At a boat canal near our motel I spent hours casting to needlefish, little bolts of quicksilver on the surface that struck the bait viciously again and again without ever getting themselves hooked. If I happened to be near deeper water, sometimes the dark shape of a barracuda would materialize, approaching a little fish I'd hooked and then palming it like a giant hand. The moment the rod folded with his weight, the ease with which the line parted, the speed with which the rod snapped back were as much of the monster as I wanted to know.

At times, catching even a single little fish has been far preferable to catching no fish at all. Often I have landed my first with relief, knowing that at least now I can say I caught something. One afternoon four friends and I rented boats to fish a Michigan pond supposedly full of bluegills and large-mouth bass. In twenty man-hours of determined fishing, be-tween us we did not catch or see a fish. One of us, however, drifting bait on the bottom, did catch a clam. About the size of a fifty-cent piece, the bivalve had closed over the hook so tightly that it required needle-nosed pliers to dislodge. Of course it was of no use to us other than as a curiosity, and did not dispel the gloom with which we rowed back to the jeering locals at the boat-rental dock. But it did reveal its usefulness later when we reported to friends and family about the day. They asked how we did, and we said, "Well, we caught a clam." Such a statement will always set non-fishermen back on their heels (*You caught a clam? Is that good?*) and defangs the scorn that awaits the fishless angler's return.

I look for fish in any likely water I see—harbors, rivers, ir-rigation ditches, hotel-lobby fountains. Every decade, maybe, I spot a long snook lurking in the shadow of a docked sailboat somebody's trying to sell, or a tail among the reeds at the edge of a pond that connects itself to a body that connects itself to a head improbably far away, or a leviathan back and dorsal fin breaching just once in the Mississippi that even today I can't believe I saw. More often, I see nothing, or little fish. The two are not so different; if a big fish is like the heart of a watershed, little fish are like the water itself. I've taken just-caught little fish and put them in the hands of children watching me from the bank, and the fish gyrate and writhe and flop their way instantly from the hands back to the water, not so much a living thing as the force that makes things live. I've spotted little fish in trickles I could step across, in basin-sized pools beneath culverts in dusty Wyoming pastures, in puddles in the woods connected to no inlet or outlet I could see—fish originally planted, I'm told, in the form of fish eggs on the feet of visiting ducks. One of the commonplaces of modern life is the body of water by the gravel pit or warehouse district where you know for a fact not even a minnow lives. The sight of just one healthy little brook trout, say, testifies for the character of the water all around, redeems it, raises it far up in our estimation.

Near where I used to live in Montana was a brush-filled creek that ran brown with snowmelt every spring, then dwindled in the summer until it resembled a bucket of water poured on a woodpile. I never thought to look in it, or even could, until one winter when I noticed a wide part, not quite a pool, by a culvert under an old logging road. Thick ice as clear and flawed as frontier window glass covered the pool, and through the ice I saw movement. I got down on my knees in the snow and looked more closely; above the dregs of dark leaves and bark fragments on the creek bottom, two small brook trout were holding in the current. Perhaps because of the ice between us, they did not flinch when I came so near I could see the black-and-olive vermiculate markings on their backs, the pink of their gills when they breathed, the tiny red spots with blue halos on their sides. They were doing nothing but holding there; once in a while they would minutely adjust their position with a movement like a gentle furling down their lengths. Self-possessed as any storied lunker, they waited out the winter in their shallow lie, ennobling this humble flow to a trout stream.

(1996)

IT'S HARD TO EAT JUST ONE

Showing off for the bridesmaids at my sister's wedding reception years ago, I caught and ate a large black cricket. Later I mentioned the incident in a book I wrote. At a talk I gave recently, someone who had read the book asked if the story was true. My sister happened to be present, so I pointed her out and told the questioner he should ask her himself. All heads swiveled to look at her where she was sitting by the aisle in the back row. "He eats bugs," she explained shortly, her lip curled in understated disgust.

Well, I do. Not all the time, of course, but sometimes, when the opportunity is at hand. And I don't think of them as bugs but as whatever specific kind of insect they happen to be. My friend Don and I are the only people I know of who have eaten insects until we were full. Those were brown drake mayflies, snatched from the surface of a northern Michigan trout river just as they hatched from their aquatic form into winged insects. They appeared in great numbers, and the fish went crazy chasing them, and somehow that afternoon instead of fishing we joined in. I could understand why the fish were acting like that: If you're into mayflies, it's hard to eat just one. I would not go so far as to call mayflies delicious, but they do have a satisfying crunch and a taste like the soft part at the bottom of a stalk of grass.

This wasn't something I started as a kid, to gross out rivals on the playground. When I was growing up, decades ago in northern Ohio, you didn't experiment too much with what you ate. You had your peanut butter and jelly and your meat and potatoes, and that was about it. I didn't even have pizza until I was fourteen. A year or two later, my cousins moved to a fancy Connecticut suburb of New York City and at Christmas sent back sophisticated presents from the East. For me, my aunt chose an assortment of gourmet snacks I'd never seen before, including a box of chocolate-covered ants and bees. They came in cubes of chocolate wrapped in red foil or silver foil, depending on the insects inside. I waited awhile before giving them a try. I didn't even know for sure if I was really supposed to. It was an unusual present for a grown-up relative to give. But I was a teenager, and the time the 1960s, and the unusual seemed to be happening every day. So what the heck—the taste was chocolate, mainly, with a chitinous crunch to it and a slight bitterness underneath. The important lesson I learned was that you can eat quite a lot of ants and bees and still be fine.

Like many discoveries of the sixties, this one had been made before. Throughout history, we humans have eaten bugs. Although they have been out of fashion in our recipes for a while now, that wasn't always so. Archaeologists who study diet in pre-Columbian America say that in parts of the West at certain times of year, grasshoppers appear to have been the staple food. The terrifying dark clouds of hoppers that descend on Western farms may have meant breakfast in earlier times. Frontier travelers in the nineteenth century reported that Indians liked to eat insects and knew how to fix them. A man named Edwin James who traveled in the Rockes in 1820 said that Snake Indian women collected a certain kind of ant from anthills in the cool of the morning when the insects were easier to catch, put the ants into a special bag, washed and cleaned them of dirt and bits of wood, put them on a flat stone, crushed them with a rolling pin, rolled them like pastry, and made them into a delicious (to the Indians) soup.

Then of course there's the insect-eating in the Bible. The dietary laws in the Old Testament book of Leviticus list as foods forbidden to eat not only the rabbit and the pig, but also such unlikely table fare as the osprey, the pelican, and the weasel. "Flying, creeping things," i.e., insects, are also generally unclean and forbidden. But a single verse makes these exceptions: "Even these of them ye may eat; the locust after his kind, and the bald locust after his kind, and the beetle after his kind, and the grasshopper after his kind." As loopholes go, that's pretty good-sized; it suggests the lawgiver was responding to a real demand. The most famous wilderness dweller of the Bible, John the Baptist, dressed in animal skins as he wandered about preaching the coming of the Messiah. His food, we are told, was locusts and wild honey. The wild honey is not a surprise, but note his choice of insect. Even living off the land, John the Baptist kept kosher—a wild man, but still a good Jewish boy.

The truth is, aside from that black cricket and the chocolate-covered ants and bees, and aside from some night crawlers (annelids, technically not insects) that I sliced up and fried to leathery inedibility, and aside from one or two others I have forgotten about, the insects in my diet have almost all been mayflies. If you know nothing about mayflies, it may be hard to understand their appeal. The "fly" in the name, for starters, is misleading; they are nothing like the house or bluebottle variety. Mayflies spend most of their lifespan underwater as swimming insects called nymphs. Their presence in a river or other freshwater is a good sign that it is well oxygenated and passably clean. They range in size from an inch and a half to almost pinhead small. Mostly in spring and summer, they come to the surface, hatch from their nymphal forms into winged insects, mate, lay eggs, and die.

Sometimes they hatch en masse, like seniors graduating or couples marrying in June. A hatch, as it's called, is one of those events when, beneath nature's customary inscrutability, you can hear her saying, "Par-r-r-r-ty!" Mayflies start to pop up on the surface of the river—first one, then a few, then more, then hundreds of them floating downstream like runaway cakes off a conveyor belt in that episode of *I Love Lucy*. New creatures in a new environment, they're dazed, and their wings are damp, and in the moments before they get their bearings and fly they're the best free lunch a fish ever had. Trout of all sizes, from minnows on up, begin to feed with a growing sense of exultation that soon draws even the wise and reticent big guys from their cover. I've seen trout pursue mayflies with splashes and fillips and show-offy flourishes of the tail, just for joy. Swallows come swooping down and take the mayflies as they float, and dragonflies hit them in the air with a little crunching zip. Robins zigzag overhead, braking so suddenly when they catch one in mid-flight that their feet skid forward in front of them. In webs along the bank, spiders wake up to a sudden windfall and hurry to subdue the captives. In the spring air, the new mayflies float and shimmer like soap bubbles. The whole scene usually makes me want to get busy and catch some fish; sometimes it makes me want to just lay back my head and open my mouth and let the bounty fall in.

Once, when I was just starting out as a reporter in New York, I attended a grossly expensive dinner to promote some movie or other. It was held at an Indian restaurant, and for the last course, after the desserts and the teas, waiters brought out linen-covered trays on top of which were small foil rectangles of silver. Silver, the metal. Waiters served each guest a sheet of foil, and then, following our hosts, we put the silver on our tongues, savored, chewed, and swallowed. Silver is not tasty— not a dessert metal, really. But eating it causes your awareness to expand, as the implications proliferate and ricochet around in your brain. You register each second of the experience; you think, "I'm eating *silver!*"

Eating mayflies is a lot like that for me. Say that I find a small, newly hatched mayfly floating down the Clark Fork River in Montana. I lift it from the surface tension with the ball of my finger. As it tries to fit its filament-fine legs among the whorls of my fingerprint, I identify it as the blue-winged olive, *Ephemerella flavilinea.* Its name alone is prettier than silver. Its wings are a semigloss, cigarette-smoke bluish gray, a color mentally delicious in itself. In my mouth, its actual taste is tiny but real, and its resistance to teeth and tongue less than a single egg of caviar. I'm part of a group that includes John the Baptist and Paleo-Indians and the Snakes of the Rockies. Like the ancients, I'm taking what the wilderness provides. I'm eating bugs, just as natural as can be.

(1997)

IN THE BRAIN

O n one of the long motoring
vacations my family used to take—five kids on a mattress in
the back of the station wagon, our parents in front sharing the
driving, heading down a highway in the Yukon Territories or
on the Canadian prairies or some other far-flung place of the
sort my father preferred—I saw my brother Dave writhing
and wincing in pain. Of the siblings, I am the oldest and Dave
the second oldest. In those days, I found certain of his suffer-
ings to be of scientific interest: on occasion, I even did what I
could to increase them just for my own information. In this
case, I observed him screwing up his features, muttering to
himself, and once in a while shaking his head like a horse in a
cloud of flies. Finally I asked him what was wrong. "I can't
stop thinking about the words 'inclined plane'!" he said. "No
matter what I do they keep running through my head: inclined
plane inclined plane inclined plane!" Our mother turned
around and tried to comfort him, suggesting that he just think
of something else, but Dave replied that trying to think of
something else only caused him to think of inclined plane

more. He sat there, beset and wretched, the golden inclined plains of Canada (or wherever) rolling past our station-wagon windows.

The day eventuated, as travel days do. We stopped at a point of interest, ate at a little restaurant in a little town, checked into a motel. After the bouncing on the beds, the putting on of pajamas, the listening to of stories read by our father, Dave and I got into one twin bed and the three younger kids into the other. As the lights went out, and our eyes adjusted to the single beam falling through the opening in the door between our parents' room and ours, a wicked realization crossed my mind. "Dave," I whispered, "*inclined plane.*" I was rewarded with a moan like the moan of the damned.

The old saying about history occurring first as tragedy and the second time as farce seems to work in reverse order for me. Jokes I make, often at someone else's expense, have a way of turning up later as real and strangely less funny problems in my own life. My brother's affliction proved to be contagious: getting a name or a phrase or a few bars of music stuck in my head has become one of the minor banes of existence for me. At certain moments I have practically prayed for a distraction to dislodge whatever happens to be stuck, much as hiccup sufferers hope for an unexpected and curative fright. For years I lived in New York City and had distractions to spare; in New York no idea survives in the mind for any length of time. But then I moved to a rural place where the distractions amounted to (1) the smell of pine needles and (2) time to put gas in the car. In such a distraction-free environment, *idées fixes* float through the air and catch in the folds of my brain like invisible wind-borne cockleburs.

One afternoon not long ago I was out fishing. The day was warm and sunny, the river clear and wadable, the fish rising.

In short, nothing about the day or the fishing conditions needed improvement. As I worked my way up a brushy bank, I saw, in a patch of light among the bushes' underwater shadows, a large rainbow trout slowly appearing. He materialized in the patch of light so clearly that I could see his greenish-gold back, his regularly spaced black speckles, the steady pulsing of his gills. In the next second he was back in the shadows, invisible again. Almost simultaneously, I became aware that I was thinking obsessively of the name Barbaralee Diamonstein-Spielvogel.

Well, that did it. I knew how the rest of my fishing afternoon would go. "Barbaralee Diamonstein-Spielvogel . . . Barbaralee Diamonstein-Spielvogel," said my brain, matching the syllables to the mechanics of my cast. I looked about hopelessly for a change of subject. With a high-pitched cry, an osprey coasted overhead, plunged down, and Barbaralee Diamonstein-Spielvogeled a fish from the shallows. The Barbaralee Diamonstein-Spielvogel ripples widened and grew. Do you know who Barbaralee Diamonstein-Spielvogel is? I'm not sure I do. She's a society person in New York, I think. Her name is as infectious as pinkeye. Running now on inertia alone, I joylessly fished through the perfect afternoon, inwardly, unstoppably praying,

> *Barbaralee Diamonstein-Spielvogel*
> *Forgive us for what we have done.*

Further, this is the kind of malady that qualifies the sufferer for no sympathy at all. That afternoon I may have caught fish or I may not; I can't remember. I know that I arrived home when I had said I would, outwardly intact, with no obvious grounds for complaint. And yet inwardly, how flummoxed I was, how vexed! What could I answer my wife and children when they asked how I had enjoyed my afternoon? "It was okay, but I couldn't stop thinking of the name Barbaralee Diamonstein-Spielvogel." Or, more honestly and more pitifully, "Help me! The name Barbaralee Diamonstein-Spielvogel is about to drive me insane!"

Studies have shown (or would show, if they existed) that among outdoor enthusiasts between the ages of forty and fifty-two who do repetitive-motion activities like rowing, long-distance cycling, jogging, or hiking, fully 37 percent have the words to the song "In-A-Gadda-Da-Vida" echoing in their brains. Those shrink-wrapped cross-country bicycle riders you see strung out for miles along state highways in the middle of the country are an internalized procession of the peskiest and most viruslike of Top 40 tunes from the past. Do you recall, by any chance, the robotic "I'm Telling You Now," by Freddie and the Dreamers? Almost certainly, cross-country bicyclists of a certain age do. The next time you see one stopped by the side of the road, pull over and roll down your window and sing a few bars of "I'm Telling You Now" for him. He may curse you and and carry it with him all the way to Minneapolis–St. Paul. On the other hand, he may thank you for driving out what had been torturing him before, a song that went something like "Why do you build me up, Buttercup, baby, just to let me down, mmmm mmmm mess me around," and so on, to which he could recall only the tune and a smattering of lyrics but not the title or the name of the group. From the brain's point of view, imperfection of memory is no obstacle. The brain runs through the little it does recall quite cheerfully and endlessly just the same. It likes the dumbest things. Why doesn't it replay great symphonies, in full one-hundred-piece orchestration? If we had only known, in the sixties, that these three-chord hit songs on the radio were going to accompany us into eternity—well, I'm sure back then we wouldn't have cared.

I carry guidebooks with me when I hike, to identify flora and fauna that catch my eye. Once identified, their names escape from me in an instant, like the names of strangers at a crowded party. Over the last year, I have learned the dog-toothed violet, the serviceberry bush, and the false morel mushroom—only a tiny percentage of all the specimens that I have looked up. Although I refer to a conifer guide when I'm cross-country skiing, I am still not trustworthy on the difference between a spruce and a fir. (Now I remember—a fir has short, flat needles and a spruce has short, pointy needles that aren't as flat. I think.) But let the smallest piece of commercial-packaging trash appear along the trail and I can give you the species, genus, and phylum every time. That fan of reflected light, for example, flickering stroboscopically in the rippling current of the creek, comes from a flattened part of a beer can on the creek bottom, a beer can that even at this distance I can identify as belonging to the genus Budweiser and the species Bud Dry.

That's the hard part: living with the realization that we have junk-filled brains. Much of the litter we bring with us into the wilderness is of the mental variety; past a certain point, our minds really cannot grasp places that are completely trash-free. The Fanta grape-soda can drawing bees in the middle of a supposedly pristine wilderness campsite provokes our outrage and disgust, of course. But underneath those feelings, and less comfortable to admit, is a small amount of recognition and even relief. The Fanta can is *us*, after all. In the nineteenth century, when the cult of the Scenic had just begun, advertisers (especially in New England) took to plastering giant advertising slogans on the scenery itself. Hikers who reached lofty lookout points in the Adirondacks or the Berkshires would see the words VISIT OAK HALL on a rock face in the prospect before them. (Oak Hall was a Boston clothing store.) Even more remarkable is how few of them seem to have complained.

The other day, while enjoying one of my two distractions—putting gas in the car—I noticed that a candy company had managed to set an advertisement into the previously neglected space between the top of the gas pump handle's grip and the base of the nozzle. It featured a full-color photograph of a candy bar and the words "Hungry? Try a ——." I wondered: If I asked, do you suppose they would buy space on the inside of my eyelids? Nowadays advertisers no longer bother to afflict the scenery. Today they think small and specific; they know that the best medium is the individual consciousness itself. With so much of our commerce trying to inveigle its tiny way into our waking and sleeping thoughts, some of it is bound to stick, adding to the random detritus, songs and phrases and floating bits of near-nonsense there already. We will never get rid of it all. We can only be thankful that it follows its own slow cycle of decay; at least we no longer murmur, as we drift off to sleep by the campfire light, "See the U.S.A. in your Chevrolet" or "Visit Oak Hall."

We can be thankful, too, that it stops with us. Most animals, for example, do not like to watch TV. What a blessing that is! Bad enough that the raccoons show up regularly to plunder the garbage cans out back; how much worse if they showed up regularly in the branches by the living-room window to catch the Thursday-night lineup on NBC. With TVs in every cage and caged animals staring at them, zoos would be even drearier places than they already are. What we have in common with the rest of nature goes deeper than advertising, deeper than words. One way to regard the annoying phrase stuck in the mind is as a boundary marking where the not-human begins. The last time I fished I caught big brown trout one after another, prehistoric-looking battlers with banana-yellow bellies and inky spots the size of dimes on their sides. Several of them jumped at me when they felt the hook, appearing suddenly in the air and fixing me with their wild eyes. As I revived them before releasing them, my two hands barely able to fit around the breadth of their sides, I looked again and again at their eyes. They held a concentrated intentionality, a consciousness I could only guess at. And yet I knew for absolute certain that (*Everybody was Kung Fu fighting*) unlike me the trout did not have the words (*Those cats were fast as lightning*) to a 1970s pop tune (*In fact it was a little bit frightening*) called "Kung Fu Fighting" (*But they fought with expert timing*) running through their brains.

(1998)

A LOVELY SORT OF

LOWER PURPOSE

As kids, my friends and I spent a lot of time out in the woods. "The woods" was our part-time address, destination, purpose, and excuse. If I went to a friend's house and found him not at home, his mother might say, "Oh, he's out in the woods," with a tone of airy acceptance. It's similar to the tone people sometimes use nowadays to tell me that someone I'm looking for is on the golf course or at the hairdresser's or at the gym, or even "away from his desk." The combination of vagueness and specificity in the answer gives a sense of somewhere romantically incommunicado. I once attended an awards dinner at which Frank Sinatra was supposed to appear, and when he didn't, the master of ceremonies explained that Frank had called to say he was "filming on location." Ten-year-olds suffer from a scarcity of fancy-sounding excuses to do whatever they feel like for a while. For us, saying we were "out in the woods" worked just fine.

We sometimes told ourselves that what we were doing in the woods was exploring. Exploring was a more prominent idea back then than it is today. History, for example, seemed to be mostly about explorers, and the semirural part of Ohio where we lived still had a faint recollection of being part of the frontier. At the town's two high schools, the sports teams were the Explorers and the Pioneers. Our explorations, though, seemed to have less system than the historic kind: something usually came up along the way. Say we began to cross one of the little creeks plentiful in the second-growth forests we frequented and found that all the creek's moisture had somehow become a shell of milk-white ice about eight inches above the now-dry bed. No other kind of ice is as satisfying to break. The search for the true meridian would be postponed while we spent the afternoon breaking the ice, stomping it underfoot by the furlong, and throwing its bigger pieces like Frisbees to shatter in excellent, war-movie-type fragmentation among the higher branches of the trees.

Stuff like that—throwing rocks at a fresh mudflat to make craters, shooting frogs with slingshots, making forts, picking blackberries, digging in what we were briefly persuaded was an Indian burial mound—occupied much of our time in the woods. Our purpose there was a higher sort of un-purpose, a free-form aimlessness that would be beyond me now. Once, as we tramped for miles along Tinker's Creek, my friend Kent told me the entire plot of two Bob Hope movies, *The Paleface* and *Son of Paleface*, which he had just seen on a double bill. The joke-filled monotony of his synopsis went well with the soggy afternoon, the muddy water, the endless tangled brush. (Afterward, when I saw the movies themselves, I found a lot to prefer in Kent's version.) The woods were ideal for those trains of thought that involved tedium and brooding. Often when I went by myself I would climb a tree and just sit.

I could list a hundred pointless things we did in the woods.

Climbing trees, though, was a common one. Often we got "lost" and had to climb a tree to get our bearings. If you read a story in which someone does that successfully, be skeptical; the topmost branches are usually too skinny to hold weight, and we could never climb high enough to see anything except other trees. There were four or five trees that we visited regularly—tall beeches, easy to climb and comfortable to sit in. We spent hours at a time in trees, afflicting the best perches with so many carved-in names, hearts, arrows, and funny sayings from the comic strips that we ran out of room for more.

It was in a tree, too, that our days of fooling around in the woods came to an end. By then some of us had reached seventh grade and had begun the bumpy ride of adolescence. In March, the month when we usually took to the woods again after winter, two friends and I set out to go exploring. Right away we climbed a tree, and soon were indulging in the spurious nostalgia of kids who have only short pasts to look back upon. The "remember whens" faltered, finally, and I think it occurred to all three of us at the same time that we really were rather big to be up in a tree. Some of us had started wearing unwoodsy outfits like short-sleeved madras shirts and penny loafers, even after school. Soon there would be the spring dances on Friday evenings in the high school cafeteria. We looked at the bare branches around us receding into obscurity, and suddenly there was nothing up there for us. Like Adam and Eve, we saw our own nakedness, and that terrible grown-up question "What are you *doing*?" made us ashamed.

We went back to the woods eventually—and when I say "we," I'm speaking demographically, not just of my friends and me. Millions of us went back, once the sexual and social business of early adulthood had been more or less sorted out. But significantly, we brought that same question with us. Now we had to be seriously doing—racing, strengthening, slimming, traversing, collecting, achieving, catching-and-releasing. A few parts per million of our concentrated purpose changed the chemistry of the whole outdoors. Even those rare interludes of actually doing nothing in the woods took on a certain fierceness as we reinforced them with personal dramas, usually of a social or sexual kind: The only way we could justify sitting motionless in an A-frame cabin in the north woods of Michigan, for example, was if we had just survived a really messy divorce.

"What are you *doing*?" The question pursues me still. When I go fishing and catch no fish, I berate myself inwardly. The pastime is seldom a relaxation for me. I must catch fish; and if I do, I must then catch more. On a Sunday afternoon last summer I took my two young children fishing with me on a famous trout stream near my house. My son was four and my daughter was eight, and I kidded myself that in their company I would be able to fish with my usual single-minded mania. I suited up in my waders and tackle-shopful of gear and led my kids from the parking area down toward the water. On the way, however, we had to cross a narrow, shallow irrigation ditch dating from when this part of the valley had farms. Well, the kids saw that little ditch and immediately took off their shoes and waded in and splashed and floated pinecones. My son got an inexplicable joy from casting his little spinning rod far over the ditch into the woods and reeling the rubber casting weight back through the trees. My daughter observed many tent caterpillars—a curse of yard owners that year— falling from bushes into the ditch and floating helplessly along, and she decided to rescue them. She kept watching the water carefully, and whenever she spotted a caterpillar she swooped down and plucked it out and put it carefully on the bank. I didn't have the heart to drag the kids away, and as I was sitting in all my fishing gear beside that unlikely trickle, a fly fisherman about my age and just as geared-up came along. He took me in at a glance, noticed my equipment and my idleness, and gave a small but unmistakable snort of derision. I was offended, but I understood how he felt as he and his purpose hurried on by.

Here, I'd like to consider a word whose meaning has begun to drift like a caterpillar on a stream. That word is "margin." Originally its meaning—the blank space around a body of type or the border of a piece of ground—had neutral connotations. But its adjective form, "marginal," now has a negative tinge. Marginal people or places or activities are ones that don't quite work out, don't sufficiently account for themselves in the economic world. From the adjective sprouted a far-fetched verb, "marginalize," whose meaning is only bad. To be marginalized is to be a victim, and to marginalize someone else is an act of exclusion that can cost you tenure. Today's so-called marginal people are the exact equivalents, etymologically, of the old-time heathens. A heathen was a savage, wild, un-Christian person who lived out on a heath. The heath was the margin of Christendom. No one today would ever use the word "heathen" except ironically, but we call certain people and activities marginal without a hint of irony all the time.

I've never been on a heath, but to judge from accounts of coal-smogged London in the days when "heathen" was in vogue, a windswept place full of heather and salmon streams sounds like the better place to be. And if the modern version of the margin is somewhere in western Nebraska, and the un-margin, the coveted red-hot center, is a site like Rodeo Drive, I wouldn't know which to choose. We need both, but especially as the world gets more jammed up, we need margins. A book without margins is impossible to read. And marginal behavior can be the most important kind. Every purpose-filled activity we pursue in the woods began as just fooling around. The first person to ride his bicycle down a mountain trail was doing a decidedly marginal thing. The margin is where you can try out odd ideas that you might be afraid to admit to with people looking on. Scientists have a term for research carried on with no immediate prospects of economic gain: "blue-sky research." Marginal places are the blue-sky-research zones of the outdoors.

Unfortunately, there are fewer and fewer of them every day. Now a common fate of a place on the margin is to have a convenience store or a windowless brick building belonging to a telephone company built on it. Across the country, endless miles of exurbia now overlap and spill into one another with hardly a margin at all. There's still a lot of open space out there, of course, but usually it's far enough from home that just getting to it requires purpose and premeditation. As the easy-to-wander-into hometown margins disappear, a certain kind of wandering becomes endangered, too.

On the far west side of the small Western city where I live, past the town-killer discount stores, is an open expanse of undeveloped ground. Its many acres border the Bitterroot River, and its far end abuts a fence surrounding a commercial gravel pit. It is a classic marginal, anything-goes sort of place, and at the moment I prefer it to just about anywhere I know.

Army reservists sometimes drive tanks there on weekends. The camouflaged behemoths slithering across the ground would make my skin crawl if I didn't suspect that the kids driving them were having such a good time. The dirt-bike guys certainly are, as they zip all over, often dawn to dusk, exuberantly making a racket. Dads bring their kids to this place to fly kites and model airplanes, people in a converted school bus camp there for weeks on end, coin-shooters cruise around with metal detectors, hunters just in off the river clean game, college kids party and leave heaps of cigarette butts and beer cans and occasionally pieces of underwear. I fish there, of course, but remarkably I don't always feel I have to. Sometimes I also pick up the trash, and I pull my kids around on a sled in the winter, and I bring friends just off the plane to sit on the riverbank and drink wine and watch the sunset.

Soon, I'm sure, Development will set its surveyor's tripod on this ground and make it get with one program or another. Rumblings of this have already begun to sound in the local newspaper. I foresee rows of condominiums, or an expansion of the gravel pit, or a public park featuring hiking trails and grim pieces of exercise equipment every twenty yards. That last choice, in all its worthy banality, somehow is the most disheartening of all. A plan will claim the empty acres and erase the spotted knapweed and the tank tracks and the beer-can heaps. The place's possibilities, which at the moment are approximately infinite, will be reduced to merely a few. And those of uncertain purpose will have to go elsewhere when they feel like doing nothing in particular, just fooling around.

(1998)

GUIDING GUYS

The beautiful McIllhenny River rises timelessly from the foot of the Rocky Mountains in the anglers' paradise that we at Pools and Riffles Guiding Service and Angling Supplies call home. Tumbling from a cleft in a fawn-colored cliff, it runs clear and cold as chilled gin across lovely rocks in headlong flight, only to spread in easy, wadable flats harboring monster brown trout if you know where to look; then it doubles back on itself the opposite way for seven miles in a blue-ribbon section where overhanging ponderosa pines dapple its surface and the play of rose-pink on the sunset ripples of the feeding pods of fish can make you wonder why you ever . . .

May I put you on hold for a second?

Hi, I'm back. Anyway, it's a river to dream of, and at Pools and Riffles, we do. I'm Steve, the owner, chief guide, and chairman of the board. Some years ago I gave up helping folks with their 401(k)'s at Crane White down in the big city. Moved here with my wife, Larissa, and never looked back once, except for the alimony thing. Been here almost two and a half years, every day kicking myself that I didn't do this sooner. The river is in my blood now, it *is* my blood itself, and I dream of it—waking and sleeping I dream of the river. (And also of hitting a small bearded man in a fedora about the head with a carrot.)

Take a look at our brochure: Pools and Riffles is just off the interstate and a short drive from Camas International Airport, with daily service to all major hubs. We'll pick you up in our special van and take you to your accommodations; or, if you choose, you can reserve our streamside lodge with all the amenities, including fax and secretarial. Whether you're an experienced fly fisherman or have a Visa card that was issued just last week, we can provide a consummate angling adventure for everyone. If you don't have your own gear, we'll be happy to rent it to you while explaining that if you're really serious you're going to wind up buying all this stuff eventually anyway so in the long run it'd be cheaper just to go ahead and buy it now. But in this, as in everything, the ultimate decision rests with you.

Maybe you live in a crowded, built-up, urban area filled with urban-type people and their hairdos and CD players. That's your business. Personally, I can take it or let it alone. Up here you'll find that the urban-type environment seems awfully far away. At Pools and Riffles our goal is to make you forget that world and immerse yourself in ours—in our pristine, crime-free streams and rivers, our clear blue skies (we get over three hundred days of sunshine a year!), and our many acres of motels where you usually never have to lock your doors.

To guarantee you the finest fly-fishing experience available, Pools and Riffles has assembled the most outstanding staff of licensed angling guides in the Rocky Mountain region. Whether you're looking for an afternoon float trip, an overnight, or even a week's excursion into the backcountry, we know we've got the perfect trout-hound for you, whatever your personal preference or style. Allow me to introduce you.

First, there's *Craig*, our resident mountain man. Craig is big—need I say more? Craig'll run about six foot seven and about 260, 275 pounds. We're talking big, and that's not even counting the beard. Craig doesn't say much. He doesn't have to—just "Yep," "Nope," and "Like some freshly ground black pepper on yer salad, hoss?" On a trout stream he can do whatever's needed, from tying a size 24 midge fly out of pocket lint to patching through a call to your broker in Tokyo on your cell phone. He practically grew up on these waters since he moved here from Seattle in '96. Wild and free as the mountains themselves, he's always happy to run back to the car and get you any little item you desire. He'll put you onto some trophy fish and himself onto a much-deserved tip, you can be sure.

Potter is from one of the oldest families on Philadelphia's Main Line, but he'd never tell you that himself. Back in the days of silk fly lines, Pot's great-granddad was the fellow who taught J. P. Morgan the double-haul. But ol' Pot's just guiding for the sport of it, and he's every bit as regular as you or me. If you've got a problem with your casting mechanics, Pot will see it right away and take care to point it out each time you cast. He's famous for encouraging his clients with old angling sayings like "I *beg* you to cast that fly to four o'clock!" and "I *can't* believe you missed that strike!" Shiny, high forehead, old-fashioned shades with side panels, big grin, bottle of Pouilly-Fumé in the cooler, Hasty Pudding anecdotes—that's Pot. Your angling education isn't complete until you've spent long hours on the water with him. Did I mention he's a gourmet cook?

Stan is by far the most dedicated trout angler you will ever meet. He lived in a sleeping bag in a cave above Twelve-Mile Reservoir for eight years, fishing with mouse patterns all night long, if that gives you any idea. His wife's the one that ran off with Claus von Bulow. Stan is in a program now and has begun to take responsibility for some of the problems from his past. Stan has learned to redirect hurtful emotions the way any sensible guy should—straight into fishing, and more fishing after that. There's not a dime's worth of "quit" in Stan.

Unlike the rest of us, *Bethany-Anne* is not a man. As the result of an amicable sex-discrimination lawsuit, we are happy to add her to the team. Despite lacking the upper-body strength required for high-wind casting and pulling the boat out of the water, Bethany-Anne can do some things. Beyond that I'm not at liberty to say. If you happen to arrive with a spouse or girlfriend or other non-fishing guest, a trip with Bethany-Anne might work out just fine.

President Jimmy Carter joined our staff last fall, and we're honored that he did. Everybody knows what an avid fly fisherman Jimmy is. Historians add that Jimmy is the first President or former President to guide. It costs a little more to fish with Jimmy, and it's worth it, too. (When you're sitting around the campfire, get him to tell you about how he shaved that Secret Service agent's head that time.) He's as personable and friendly and laid-back as they come, just so long as you don't lose any of his tackle or get cigarette ashes in the boat or anything. Jimmy may be the only recent President never to have been indicted, but don't let the record fool you: He can outsmart anything that swims. As you shake his hand goodbye at the end of a once-in-a-lifetime angling epic, remember that the customary gratuity for former heads of state is 33 percent. Gentlemen, we give you the President!

A word of advice, just between us: During the months of June through October, our bookings are usually very heavy, so it's a good idea to schedule far in advance. To help with your plans, Pools and Riffles has set up its own toll-free number predicting stream flows and fishing conditions for the next five years. A taped announcement of upcoming conditions indicates what you can expect on the dates you have in mind: Condition 1 (Best Fishing I've Ever Seen), Condition 2 (Best Fishing in Twenty Years), Condition 3 (Excellent, Excellent Fishing), Condition 4 (Great Fishing, for This Time of Year), Condition 5 (The Guys Have Been Catching Some Great Fish), and Condition 6 (Great Fishing, Far as I Know, So C'mon Up!).

Occasionally we get questions from potential clients about the incidence of whirling disease in local waters and its possible consequences in a sharp decline in trout populations. However, according to a study we have read, the latest data indicate that there is no such thing as whirling disease.

Out West, the federal government puts out a lot of this misinformation in order to collect its confiscatory taxes and keep down the number of fishing guides. (We offer discounts for payments in cash!) As far as we're concerned, the best people to manage a resource are working anglers who see the river year in and year out, not some bureaucrats somewhere. In our effort to promote wise use, we practice a strict but voluntary policy of catch-and-release. This means that every fish caught will be measured, weighed, photographed, recorded with a tracing of its outline on butcher paper, and returned to the river so that it can have the same experience another day. If this offends the meat fisherman, so be it; no angler we'd care to fish with would do otherwise.

Many of our clients keep coming back to us year after year, we find. All kinds of folks head our way—they're middle-aged, approaching middle age, or in their forties or fifties or mid-fifties; gray-haired, balding, or having not very much gray hair; they might be doctors, lawyers, entertainment attorneys, physicians, bankers, stockbrokers, accountants with law degrees, or surgeons. What they share, and what we at Pools and Riffles prize, is an infectious enthusiasm for being out on the river with a fly rod and fishing and laughing in a particular way just all the time.

At Pools and Riffles we understand that the quality of the angling experience doesn't depend on how many fish you catch, so long as you catch a lot, but rather on their size and on nobody else's being bigger. Such incidentals are the trophies we truly treasure. The light sparkling on the wet clothes of a friend who fell in, the disappointed expression on the face of your partner when you land one, or the complimentary beer in the late afternoon by the boat launch with the car radio playing as you sign the receipt—these are the intangibles. This is what we offer at Pools and Riffles, where the finest in fly-fishing is as near as a few phone calls, cab ride, an airport, another airport, a third airport, and a courtesy van ride away.

(1999)

FISHING IN TOWN

I used to fish in the East River in New York City. Lots of people do. On a sunny fall day its almost-clear waters glint with baitfish, which sometimes boil to the surface when chased by deeper-swimming bluefish and striped bass. Fly-casting saltwater streamers, I hit streetlamps with my backcast. On October mornings I flung heavy lead-head jigs with a surf-casting rod far into the oceanic currents under the Manhattan Bridge. I penciled my fishing in among work and family responsibilities. I could be fishing for stripers on the Lower East Side before sunup and get back to Brooklyn to take care of the kids by breakfast time.

It would have been bad if I had been late. Angling lore is short on advice about this aspect of the sport: basically, your family and friends would prefer that you didn't do it. There's a deep lonesome willfulness to it that just isn't sociable at all. I find that even when family and friends join me, they want to fish where I don't want to, in a way I don't want to, beginning and ending when I don't want to. I remember reading once about a guy who drove taxis in Boston in the winter and spent the rest of the year living in a station wagon out West some-where so he could fish completely distraction-free. I believe that is the kind of angling holiness one should aspire to. Un-fortunately, it would destroy any emotional life you had in about seventeen days. A trick of angling as important as wet vs. dry or the Leisenring Lift is how to pursue the sport satis-factorily without making your family too mad. In former times, maybe we would not mention this dilemma, for fear of appearing wimpy; but nowadays we can admit that's just the way it is. A good solution I have found is to fish as I learned to in New York—right in town.

All cities don't have fishing as good as New York's, but they should. People like to live near water, so they and fish are natural neighbors. If a city or town has shoreline but no fish-ing of any kind, something's wrong. How can you trust a place like that? The fishing doesn't have to be fancy or pris-tine, so long as it exists. For example, I thought more highly of Cincinnati after a recent trip there when I strolled along the strip of shore between the Ohio River and the concrete cliffs supporting the Riverfront Stadium parking garage and I met some still-fishermen, and one told me that a few nights before he had caught a near-record blue catfish at that spot. I asked what he had used for bait, and he said half a White Castle french fry.

When I moved from New York, I chose a small Western city where the fishing is great. Sportfishing here is a medium-sized industry with a multiplicity of fly shops and guide ser-vices and hotel packages for anglers. In late summer they pour off the connecting flights from Salt Lake City or Minneapo-lis–St. Paul, fishing fever in their eyes. But evidently what they've been dreaming of all year in their perhaps congested hometowns isn't the productive stretch of riverfront I know about next to the lot for Les Schwab Tires, where the outdoor address system occasionally rasps, "Horst, you have a call on line one." No, they want to get away from Les Schwab Tires and its highway-strip ilk, understandably, so they head for wilder places not far off. This means that in town, even at the peak of the season, often you can cast to rising fish for hours without another fisherman to be seen.

Not that the river or its banks are deserted. For starters people live here, off and on, and set up mini-camps in the bushes. Once, I came out of a slow pool pinstriped on its surface with the reflection of power lines overhead and nearly brought my wading shoe down on a washcloth, toothbrush, and tube of toothpaste laid out neatly in a row on a shoreline rock. I've encountered clothes, and occasional furniture. On hot days, people set up lawn chairs in the shallows. Weekends, crowds of floating recreationists on inner tubes or rafts go by practically every five minutes. An angling friend says that if the fish in town stopped feeding every time a floater went by, they'd starve to death. I have been offered beers, and plenty of advice, from the passing flotilla. A guy speed-paddling a canoe almost ran me down. And then there was the woman in the bikini on an air mattress going over the little falls at the weirs. My friend once fished all the way through the city limits from west to east and wrote a series about the experience for the local paper. He was stopped in his upstream progress by policemen in chest waders searching for a murder suspect who had ducked out the back way of a motel and holed up on a little island in the river. They caught her, and she got life in prison. I think of her every time I fish there.

My favorite place these days is out by the golf course on the edge of town. Last summer I caught one of the biggest trout of my life in the deep water at the riprap below the seventeenth green. I had gone out for just an hour or so, in an idling mood, intending to fool around with a lightweight rod I hadn't used in years. Grasshoppers were everywhere, so I found a beat-up hopper in the fleece of my vest, tied it on, and cast to some rises upstream. It sank; there was a turmoil under the surface, the line pulled tight, and a rainbow made a long horizontal leap toward shore. Then he did a kick-turn like in a swim meet and sped for the deepest water in mid-river. Immediately the fly line—I had no backing—shrank to a few coils left on the spool, the rod tip was dowsing toward the surface like mad, and I was splashing downstream among the riprap. For a while he held still, the line vibrating. Two people drifted past in a raft, and the fish suddenly jumped high next to it and fell back broadside with a whumping splash like a thrown dictionary. More minutes followed. Finally he came swooning to my net, and I took him to a triangular-shaped piece of water among the rocks and measured him against my rod, which he seemed to be about half the length of. I revived him there, balancing him upright with my fingertips, almost embarrassed at my luck, at his size, at the otherwise-ordinariness of the day. Golfers continued to play, oblivious, not ten feet above me. They were talking about whose turn it was to putt; one said, "I think you're away."

The next thing I knew, I was home. My wife and children were doing just what they had been before I left. My wife says she can tell at first glance or by the sound of my voice whether I've caught a fish, so she knew I had. But how to convey that I'd caught a personal-record, immense, tail-walking wild rainbow out there by the seventeenth green? I tried; the commotion attracted the children: "What happened?" "Daddy caught a big fish." "Where is it?" "He let it go." "Oh." And they returned to *Darkwing Duck*. An advantage of fishing someplace far from home is that there's plenty of time, during the anticipation going and especially during the recap coming back, for a big fish to assume its proper proportions in your mind. When I had pictured catching the biggest trout of my life, I hadn't expected it would arrive unremarkably in the midst of daily occurrence, like the mail.

Rivers with good fishing are prettier than rivers without. Sometimes I have passed by pieces of water I knew were dead, and I could hardly stand to look at the fraud of light glittering on their ripples. But knowing how many fish this river holds causes me to keep a respectful eye on it as I'm doing errands nearby, even when the possibility of fishing is remote—in winter, when the river is a conveyor moving odd lots of ice, or when the temperature suddenly drops to 20 below and wraiths of steam hop from it, or when a cold spell lasts for weeks and it almost freezes over, leaving a crevice in the middle through which you can see the fast-flowing water below. Then, after ice-out in the spring, the river picks up speed until it's running ten miles an hour of brown torrent bank to bank, so full it piles back on itself in rapids of brown foam, and the glare off its surface reminds me of several recent news stories about those unfortunates it has drowned. Then the swelling subsides and the water starts to clear, and again people peer into it like kingfishers from the pedestrian walkways along the bridges.

This river, and another that runs into it nearby, made the level valley the city sits on. They used gravel, which they now cut their way through. In town, the roads and buildings are up on the gravel banks, and the river is below; the arrangement suggests the verticality of ecosystems and the dependence of the high upon the low. You're reminded of this at almost every corner, where someone has painted stencils of fish on the sidewalk above the storm drain, along with a warning that whatever goes down the drain ends up in the river. Always, the end of a fishing day in town means a climb up from the river world into paved civilization. I often fish by an industrial gravel pit where various machines stack river gravel into heaps and onto trucks. When the wind is right, dust blows from the pit onto the river, leaving a slick; during the day, the noise of engines rises and falls. But the banks are twenty or thirty feet high, the water is deep and slow, and the trout are in the twenty-inch range.

Last summer I went there many nights after dinner. This is a pool that everyone knows about, so the fish see a lot of anglers. Even the whitefish and squawfish here are selective and the rainbow trout's knowledge of fly patterns is postdoctorate. One evening I tied on fly after fly while rises splashed like hailstones all around me. That kind of can't-win-for-losing situation is addictive to me, and I kept at it until full dark. Then the rises began to taper off, and bats went by clicking like Geiger counters, and a manifestation in the air above gave me a start, until I connected it to the silhouette of a heron rising into the lighter sky above the tree line. I climbed back to my car trailed by minor rockslides, and I took off my waders and vest and headed for home. Now points of red shone from the radio towers on the peaks encircling the valley, and a glow from the city spilled upward onto the mountains like light from an orchestra pit before the curtain goes up. I drove slowly through the warm air with the windows down. The hiss of a lawn sprinkler announced the outskirts of a residential district; less-important traffic signals had been switched to flashing mode. When I pulled into my drive I saw that lights were still on in my children's bedroom. I had missed reading to them, but would still be able to say good-night. I felt a complex pleasure, the sort that is said to be provided by following rules of meter and rhyme. Here, as everywhere, ecosystems interlocked.

(1999)

FROM WILDERNESS

TO WAL-MART

Near my house, in a small city in Montana, is a creek called Pattee Creek. I pass by it often, on my way to the supermarket or the dentist's office. It runs through a ditch between front yards and the street, through a cement channel, into a small marsh behind the dentist's office, and through a culvert at the other side of the marsh. It comes out of a canyon called Pattee Canyon, a fold in the mountains that encircle the town. People around here seldom think about the creek except during the time of spring runoff, when suddenly it arrives chocolate brown and foaming and full, piling up at the culvert at Higgins Avenue like carpet skidded on the floor. At such times it is liable to flood whole neighborhoods of yards and basements. City workers watch it warily and measure its flow with metal tape measures; sandbags go on sale at the Army-Navy store.

Often, while that is happening, the mountains where Pattee Creek begins are still snow-covered and linen white. Leaning back in the dentist's chair, I can see them gleaming in the far distance. Pattee Creek extends from there almost to here; from near-wilderness to my dentist's back door.

In the spring of 1997 the snowpack in the mountains was twice as deep as usual. During warm spells people braced for the runoff, and the local paper ran headlines like HERE IT COMES! Sap dripped from maple tree branches broken by the wind; crocuses grouped like flights of darts along the sidewalks; and a general restlessness set in. The city waited, like an apartment building where men are lowering a grand piano down the stairs. As the number of watchers along the rising margins of Pattee Creek grew, I sometimes joined them. I can watch flowing water for any amount of time. Also, I like to mess around creeks. I find them companionable—flowing water of just the right scale. As the spring progressed and the snows unlocked, I rambled along the whole course of Pattee Creek, from the culvert by the parking lot at Wal-Mart to the mountaintop twenty miles away.

MARCH 21

I want to know where all this water is coming from. I drive up Pattee Canyon Road, which winds and narrows up the canyon, jumping the creek again and again on its way. I continue beyond where the sidewalk stops, past the farthest lawn, up into the colder canyon air. Here the creek tumbles through a melting and pockmarked mini-canyon of snow and gravel, the ruins of the berm the snowplow left alongside the road. I pull into a state-forest parking area and get out and walk. A mile or so farther up the road, the berm has not yet melted and still completely covers the creek. The berm is as high as my head, still its old midwinter self, a tough amalgam of snow and ice and road sand and oil and beer cans and muffler parts and yellow paint chips from the no-passing stripe. It looks like a collaboration between man and nature that nothing can destroy. I lean against it at full length and press my ear against its gritty chill. From far underneath, Pattee Creek is a dim, insistent murmur.

Today, in my search for the creek's source, this is the best I can do. The snow that looked so white from the valley is actually old and winter-worn. Here and there an unsullied snowfield rises in a shaded part of the mountain like the tail fin of a giant airplane. But under the trees the snow is furry with pine needles and bits of moss, and it grabs the ankles soggily. About every third step, I fall through to my waist—so forget it. Ribs of a winter-killed deer sit atop a snow patch, neat as the beginning of a sailboat model. From the base of a snowbank in the sun, meltwater issues in a wide, flat sheet.

MARCH 31

Along the course of the creek through town, sandbags are everywhere. In some of the low-lying neighborhoods, sandbag emplacements laid neatly on the property lines give houses a military air. The city has diverted part of the creek onto a public park, where it rises shin-deep in the baseball field; other than that, no serious flooding so far.

Up in the canyon, plenty of snow remains. In open, sunny places, clear meltwater flows with no visible bed across the pine-needle floor. Thin sheets of water run over the road, now one way, now the other, and riffle in the potholes. A capillary web of little streams connects and connects again, gurgling from a dozen little canyons down to the main creek. On the surface of a pool where a tributary joins, a pinwheel of foam turns like a hurricane seen from the air. Helmeted bicyclists whir past, stripes of mud spattered up their bright-yellow backs.

APRIL 14

My wife drops me off at the trailhead in the canyon, as near as I can get to the top of the creek's watershed. The snow has shrunk back into the places of deepest shade, and walking is easier. I follow the creek up and up, taking the larger branch every time it divides. Soon the flow is a two-foot-wide streamlet coming down one rut or another of a logging road through a ponderosa forest. I'm high up now, and breathing hard; ridge light beckons ahead.

At a switchback in the logging road, the streamlet ends in a wet patch around an upwelling of water the size of a serving platter: a spring. On the bare mountainside above are two or three smaller wet patches, each draining into the one below it. From the topmost seep, a wetness of black mud marbled with tan sand, about ten inches across, flows a noiseless trickle the width of a braided belt. And from there on up, the ground is completely dry. This, multiplied, is the source of Pattee Creek.

I continue to the ridgetop just beyond, scaring up a grouse whose wings make a sound like sails luffing in a stiff breeze. On the ridgetop, to my surprise, is another logging road. From it the view to the east, away from the city, is vast—a wooded canyon crossed with powerlines, more mountains, and far silver-blue snow clouds piled high. A squirrel chatters, dropping pinecone shards through the branches. A chickadee sings. To the west, amid the woodsmoke- and smog-blurred cityscape spread out below, a speck of light flashes, maybe from the windshield of a turning car.

I walk all the way back down to the city. Going this direction is more pleasant—I can see why water prefers it. It's two hours of walking to the first red-winged blackbird song, two and a half to the first redwood deck and barbecue grill. On the front stoop of a streamside house, a woman turns, holds up a paper sack, and asks someone behind the closed screen door, "Now, you're sure you don't want these sweetbreads?" It's about a three-hour walk to there.

APRIL 24

Still, the water comes. In town, Pattee Creek splashes along its concrete channel night and day. People who live by it must be getting tired of listening to it. A gray-haired woman in hip boots eyes it from her yard, while another woman stands by a culvert with a garden rake, ready to fish out obstructing pieces of trash. The only place the creek seems to pause in its entire course is in the marsh behind the dentist's office. Here it tops off the marsh's connecting ponds right to their grassy rims with water the color of coffee and cream. Ducklings zip across the surface, their paddle-wheeling feet a blur. A pair of muskrats work the margins; last year's cattails disintegrate to down; birdsong rises. Streets and buildings enclose the marsh on all sides, and no doubt would cover it over if they could. Too expensive and troublesome to fill in, this ignored little wetland survives.

For the creek, it's still a long way to the river. Emerging from the marsh's outflow it reassumes its character, keeping to a single channel for a couple of blocks past an apartment building, a self-storage place, and a condominium development. Then it comes to a headgate and splits into several smaller channels that dodge under fences and across back yards like a bunch of kids running from the police. The channel I follow goes down alleys, between houses, under a nakeshift plank bridge on which someone has written "Tyler is in trouble," right by a basement window with video-game controls and a tissue box on the sill, past traffic lights, under the apron of a Surejam convenience store, behind a store that sells hot tubs, and along the railroad tracks leading south out of town.

This is the city-limits zone, of discount stores spread amoebalike on the horizon and sky-high gas station signs. The stream crosses under the tracks, running now through a bed that is like a rain gutter between the railroad and a four-lane highway. The highway and the tracks begin to rise and the streambed to descend. As tires bump on the steel joint of a highway bridge, the stream beside it goes over a ledge, down a fifteen-foot grade of jumbled rock, and into the Bitterroot River.

We have reached the mouth of Pattee Creek—or of the bureaucratized, channelized subsection represented here. Its water arrives tumbling and foaming, sending bubbles in a slow upstream eddy along the shore. The eddy bends out toward the main current, and the Bitterroot, flowing full and fast, speeds it away. When the bubbles burst, they leave rings on the moving surface that lose their circularity like smoke rings in a breath of air. On ahead is the Clark Fork River, Pend Oreille Lake, the Columbia River, and the Pacific Ocean.

Much of the natural world now resembles Pattee Creek. It coexists with pavement; it goes about its business usually unnoticed; and it has a reputation as a nuisance. It's the moles in the lawn, the black ice on the interstate, the sinkage under the patio. For some reason, I prefer it to nature of the more remote and pristine kind. At least on the shores of Pattee Creek, I don't fear that my very presence is making it less pristine.

As the runoff went on and on—through May, through June—it showed its disregard for popular opinion. We wanted it over; the mountains were like a stadium parking lot taking forever to empty out. Luckily, there was never a big surge of flooding, no great hot spells or rains; most of the basements in my neighborhood stayed dry. The Pattee Creek drainage was mostly clear by mid-May, but elsewhere in the mountains the snows hung on. The rivers by the end of June were still too high and muddy to fish in. The Forest Service said that the high flows had undermined many streambanks and that people should stay off them. I ignored this warning; while kneeling to free a fishing lure stuck on a root just below the waterline, I felt the entire bank beneath me give. I went with it, clear over my head into the Bitterroot River. I could not believe that on the twenty-third of June any water could be so turbid or so cold.

Because of all the moisture, wildflowers spread over the slopes of Pattee Canyon a minute after the snows were gone. Buttercups bloomed along the creekbed all the way from the heights to where it meets the river, and at some point yellow flag irises escaped from a garden to join them. The yellow flags were still blooming along a ditch bank in July, when Pattee Creek had dwindled to a ribbon of water, clearer than air, that you had to part the streamside grasses to find.

(1998)

BAD ADVICE

Some years ago, on a camping trip in the pine woods of northern Michigan, my friend Don brought along a copy of an outdoor cookbook that appeared on the best-seller lists at the time. This book contained many ingenious and easy-sounding recipes; one that Don especially wanted to try was called Breakfast in a Paper Bag. According to this recipe, you could take a small paper lunch sack, put strips of bacon in the bottom, break an egg into the sack on top of the bacon, fold down the top of the sack, push a stick through the fold, hold the sack over hot coals, and cook the bacon and egg in the sack in about ten minutes.

I watched as Don followed the directions exactly. Both he and I remarked that we would naturally have thought the sack would burn; the recipe, however, declared, "Grease will coat the bottom of the bag as it cooks." Somehow we both took this to mean that the grease, counterintuitively, actually made the bag less likely to burn. Marveling at the "who would have guessed" magic of it, we picked a good spot in the hot coals of our campfire, and Don held the sack above them. We watched. In a second and a half, the bag burst into leaping flames. Don was yelling for help, waving the bag around trying to extinguish it, scattering egg yolk and smoldering strips of bacon and flaming paper into the combustible pines while people at adjoining campfires stared in horror and wondered what they should do.

The wild figures that the burning breakfast described in midair as Don waved the stick, the look of outraged, imbecile shock reflected on our faces—those are images that stay with me. I replay the incident often in my mind. It is like a parable. Because a book told us to, we attempted to use greased paper as a frying pan on an open fire. For all I know, the trick is possible if you do it just so; we never repeated the experiment. But to me the incident illustrates a larger truth about our species when it ventures out-of-doors. We go forth in abundant ignorance, near-blind with fantasy, witlessly trusting words on a page or a tip a guy we'd never met before gave us at a sporting-goods counter in a giant discount store. About half the time, the faith that leads us into the outdoors is based on advice that is half-baked, made up, hypothetical, uninformed, spurious, or deliberately, heedlessly bad.

Greenland, for example, did not turn out to be very green, Viking hype to the contrary. Despite what a Pawnee or Wichita Indian told the Spanish explorer Francisco Vásquez de Coronado, there were no cities of gold in western Kansas, no canoes with oarlocks made of gold, no tree branches hung with little gold bells that soothed the king (also nonexistent) during his afternoon nap; a summer's march on the Great Plains in piping-hot armor presumably bore these truths upon the would-be conquistador in an unforgettable way. Lewis and Clark found no elephants on their journey, though President Jefferson, believing reports from the frontier, had said they should be on the lookout for them. And then there was Lansford W. Hastings, the adventurer and promoter of Sacramento, purveyor of some of the worst advice of all time. He told the prospective wagon-train emigrants to California that he had discovered a shortcut (modestly named the Hastings Cutoff) that reduced travel time by many days. Yes, it did cross a few extra deserts and some unusually high mountain ranges; the unfortunate Donner Party read Hastings's book, followed his route, and famously came to its grisly end below the narrow Sierra pass that now bears its name. According to local legend, the air in the Utah foothills is still blue from the curses that emigrants heaped on Lansford W. Hastings along the way.

People will tell you just any damn thing. I have found this to be especially so in establishments called Pappy's, Cappy's, Pop's, or Dad's. The wizened, senior quality of the names seems to give the people who work in such places a license to browbeat customers and pass on whatever opinionated misinformation they please. When I go through the door of a Pappy's or Cappy's—usually it's a fishing-tackle shop, a general store, or a bar—usually there's a fat older guy sitting behind the counter with his T-shirt up over his stomach and his navel peeking out. That will be Pappy, or Cappy. Sometimes it's both. Pappy looks at me without looking at me and remarks to Cappy that the gear I've got on is too light for the country at this time of year, and Cappy agrees, crustily; then I ask a touristy, greenhorn question, and we're off. Cappy, backed by Pappy, says the rig I'm driving won't make it up that Forest Service road, and I'm headed in the wrong direction anyhow, and the best place to camp isn't where I'm going but far in the other direction, up top of Corkscrew Butte, which is closed now, as is well known.

What's worse is that I crumble in this situation, every time. I have taken more wrong advice, have bought more unnecessary maps, trout flies, water filtration devices, and assorted paraphernalia from Pappys and Cappys with their navels showing than I like to think about. Some essential element left out of my psychic immune system causes me always to defer to these guys and believe what they say. And while the Lansford W. Hastings type of bad advice tells people they can do things they really can't, the Cappy-Pappy type of advice is generally the opposite. Cappy and Pappy have been sitting around their failing store for so long that they are now convinced you're a fool for trying to do anything at all.

Complicating matters still further is Happy. She used to be married to Cappy but is now married to Pappy, or vice versa. Happy has missing teeth and a freestyle hairdo, and she hangs out in the back of the store listening in and irritatedly yelling statements that contradict most of what Pappy and Cappy say. The effect is to send you out the door as confused as it is possible to be. What's different about Happy, however, is that eventually she will tell you the truth. When you return your rented bicycle or rowboat in the evening, Pappy and Cappy are packed away in glycolene somewhere and Happy is waiting for you in the twilight, swatting mosquitoes and snapping the elastic band of her trousers against her side. You have found no berries, seen no birds, caught no fish; and Happy will tell you that the birds were right in front of the house all afternoon, the best berry bushes are behind the snow-machine shed, and she herself just caught fifty fish right off the dock. She will even show you her full stringer, cackling, "You gotta know the right place to go!"

Of course, people usually keep their best advice to themselves. They'd be crazy not to, what with all the crowds tramping around outdoors nowadays. I can understand such caution, in principle; but I consider it stingy and mean when it is applied to me. There's a certain facial expression people often have when they are withholding the one key piece of information I really need. They smile broadly with lips shut tight as a Mason jar, and a cheery blankness fills their eyes. This expression irks me to no end. Misleading blather I can put up with, and even enjoy if it's preposterous enough; but smug, determined silence is a posted sign, a locked gate, an unlisted phone. Also, I think it's the real message behind today's deluge of information-age outdoor advice, most of which seems to be about crampons, rebreathers, and synthetic sleeping bag fill. What you wanted to know does not appear. Especially in the more desirable destinations outdoors, withheld advice is the most common kind.

I craved good advice one summer when I fished a little-known Midwestern river full of brown trout. Every few days I went to the local fly-fishing store and asked the guys who worked there where in the river the really big fish I had heard about might be. The guys were friendly, and more than willing to sell me stuff, but when I asked that question I met the Mason-jar expression I've described. I tried being winsome; I portrayed myself as fishless and pitiable, told jokes, drank coffee, hung around. On the subject of vital interest, nobody offered word one.

I halfway gave up and began driving the back roads aimlessly. Then, just at sunset one evening, I suddenly came upon a dozen or more cars and pickups parked in the high grass along a road I'd never been on before. I pulled over, got out, and crashed through the brush to investigate. There, in a marshy lowland, was a section of river I had never tried, with insects popping on its surface and monster brown trout slurping them down and fly rods swishing like scythes in the summer air. Among the intent anglers along the bank I recognized the fishing-store owner's son, one of the Mason-jar-smiling regulars. The experience taught me an important outdoor fact: Regardless of what the people who know tell you or don't tell you, an off-road gathering of parked cars doesn't lie.

In case you're wondering, this particular good fishing spot was on the Pigeon River near the town of Vanderbilt, Michigan, upstream from the dam. It's been years since I fished there, so I can't vouch for the up-to-dateness of my information. But unlike smarter outdoorsmen, I am happy to pass along whatever I can, because I myself am now gabby and free with advice to an embarrassing degree. I noticed the change as I got older; I hit my mid-forties, and from nowhere endless, windy sentences of questionable advice began coming out of me. An old-guy voice takes on its own momentum, and I seem unable to stop it even when I have no idea what I'm talking about. Sometimes when strangers ask me for directions on a hiking trail or just around town, I give detailed wrong answers off the top of my head rather than admit I don't know. When my hearers are out of sight, my reason returns and I realize what I've done. Then I make myself scarce, for fear that they will discover my ridiculousness and come back in a rage looking for me.

Outdoor magazines I read as a child featured authoritative fellows in plaid shirts and broad-brimmed hats who offered sensible tips about how to find water in the desert by cutting open cacti, how to make bread from cattail roots, or how to predict the weather by the thickness of the walls of muskrat dens. I wish I had down-to-earth wisdom like that to impart, but when I search my knowledge, all that comes to mind is advice that would cause me to run and hide after I gave it. The one piece of real advice that I do have is not outdoor advice, strictly speaking; I think, however, that its soundness makes up for that drawback. It is true virtually every time, in all lands and cultures. I offer it as the one completely trustworthy piece of advice I know, and it is this: Never marry a man whose nickname is "The Killer."

Other than that, you're on your own.

(1999)

CATCHING MONSTERS

AFTER DARK

The biggest fish come out at night—or so I have believed, ever since I was a teenager and began to be abroad a lot in the night myself. At sixteen I used to stroll from my grandmother's house in Key West down to the shrimp-boat docks just after sunset and watch tarpon bigger than me swim around among the pilings eating shrimp scraps. They were like sea monsters, with their scale-plated sides shining under the dock's mercury lights, gulping and breaching in the black water an arm's length away. Once, I brought a deep-sea rod with the intention of casting a tarpon plug to them; but as their tails carelessly slapped the sides of the shrimp boats, I got an idea of the close-range violence that would follow and I didn't make a cast.

Sometimes with a girl cousin about my age I would borrow my grandmother's car and drive at night to a highway bridge north of town to watch barracuda. Usually one or two of these long, narrow, crocodile-smiling fish would be waiting below a streetlight in the brightly lit water right beside the bridge's deep shadow. On the fisherman's catwalk we stood above them; now and then one of the barracuda would shoot forward like a bolt and then slowly return to his former position with his jaws chomping. I told my cousin that the barracuda were grabbing little fish that had come out from the bridge's shadow and had not yet adjusted their eyes to the light. I was right, for all I knew—why else would the barracuda choose to hunt there?—but I offered this explanation with all the bogus confidence guys like to assume on dates.

I'm old and married now, but I still pursue fish at night. Some summers I do most of my fishing only after the sun goes down. Fishing at night still holds a teenage excitement for me, a keyed-up anticipation of the unpredictable rendezvous waiting out there somewhere in the dark.

It's scarier, too, than fishing during the day. Some years ago a fly-fishing magazine had on its cover a photo of a giant brown trout a man had caught night-fishing on a Pennsylvania stream. The hooked fish, apparently too big to lift out of the water for the picture, gaped halfway above the surface in the beam from the angler's headlamp; the trout's upper jaw was cantilevered inside like a church, and its round gold-and-black eye stared back, glittering and nocturnal and malign.

That photo, spooky as it was, inspired me to take nighttime fishing much more seriously. Not long after I saw it, I went on a fishing trip with friends on the Pigeon River in northern Michigan. One night, as my tentmates were crawling into their sleeping bags, I suited up with waders and gear and set out in the buzzing darkness of late summer to catch a monster of my own. By flashlight I followed a streamside trail and then stopped at a deep pool where I knew a big brown trout had to be. I sat on the rocks beside the water and bent down with my flashlight in my mouth and began to tie on a fly, and as my lit-up fingers were moving in the intricacies of the knot, suddenly a big mouth lunged from the darkness and bit me on the side of the hand. I yelped, kicked over my fly box, sent the flashlight flying, and ran away up the bank. After a few minutes of deep breathing, I found the flashlight and investigated. Close to where I had been sitting the light picked out a squat toad about the size of a small teapot; my fingers moving in the light no doubt had looked like food to him. I got well away, tied on my fly, and waded into the stream, but my nerves were shot and my heart wasn't in it. I could still feel the coldness of that toadmouth on my skin. After a few casts I headed gratefully to bed.

I kept on trying, though. I spent many late nights on the water, summer and fall. On the Yellowstone River in Montana I fished some nights in darkness so murky I could hardly see the end of my fly rod, let alone the bushy White Wulff dry fly I had on. The biggest challenge at first was wading into that river's strong current more or less blind. (Of course, I had scouted the water beforehand in daylight.) Fishing with so little sensory information to go on was an act of faith; casting, letting the fly drift, and casting again became odd ceremonial gestures. Staying focused was a problem. And then, as I picked up the fly at the end of a drift, something huge grabbed it. The feeling was as if a dream had reached from the darkness and yanked hard on my arm. We battled frenziedly, in complete and mutual confusion, me spinning around and nearly falling in the current, the fish pulling with electrified desperation in one direction and then another. I never saw a glimpse of him, not even a splash or the ripples of his wake.

After a short, endless time, he bent the hook out and got away. I remember him better than fish I've landed.

Sometimes I run into other night-fishing guys. On the beach at Sandy Hook on the New Jersey shore one fall there were hundreds of us assembled in the predawn hours, fishing for striped bass. All along the pale line of surf you could see us, vaguely human-shaped presences slightly darker than the sand. We passed one another on the beach, sometimes quite closely, with no sign of recognition, like sleepwalkers ghosting through a dreamscape in which each was alone.

This etiquette of the sleepwalker also applies on Western trout streams, I found. Guys—night anglers are usually guys— would appear from the darkness, move past me, and fade away without a sound other than the clicking of stones beneath their feet. Only back at the cars, illuminated by the headlights as we showed one another our catches, did we become three-dimensional beings again and regain the use of our tongues.

Naturally, the conversations never went much beyond fish and fishing. Personal subjects, such as why we were out there in the middle of the night in the first place, didn't come up. I could tell, though, that most of the nighttime anglers were middle-aged family men like me. I noticed infant-restraining seats in the backs of their vehicles or pink plastic bottles of children's strawberry-scented sunblock on the dashes. I guessed that they, like me, had become nocturnal because of the forces of domestic life. They had no doubt discovered that if you return from a pleasant afternoon on the river to find the washing machine overflowing, the kids crying, and a bunch of relatives about to arrive, then you will be in for some unhappy discussions with your wife, and on the losing end of them, as well. But if you leave to go fishing with everyone tucked safely in bed and return after midnight with them still sleeping, you're free and clear. Plus you feel harmlessly sneaky, which is always important in a marriage.

Fishing at night on the Bitterroot River near Missoula, Montana: during the last several summers I've developed a routine. I do the dishes, read to my daughter, say good-night, load my gear in the car, and go. My favorite fishing spot is a twelve-minute drive away, alongside a commercial gravel pit whose chain-link fence the river is always undercutting and dragging away. The water there is deep and powerful. Upstream from the fence is an overhanging bank on which I can perch right above feeding trout (one advantage of fishing at night is how close you can get to the fish). Within earshot, beyond some trees in the direction of town, is an outdoor theater that features musical comedies, and sometimes I hear the faint sounds of the show's finale just as the moon begins to rise. The disk of the moon's reflection slides around on the ripples of the current, making indecipherable scribbles like the tip of a lighted pen. Then sometimes in the reflection little fissures begin to appear, each accompanied by a tiny sucking pop—big rainbow and cutthroat trout are feeding on floating mayflies. I dangle my fly in the vicinity of the reflection, and whenever I hear a pop, I pull the line. Every once in a while the hook makes contact and a heavy trout suddenly threshes the surface, shattering the reflection to fragments, and then races across the river, taking line and leaping in spray that glows with a dim phosphorescence in the moonlight.

Or for variety I go to my second-favorite spot, which is a twenty-minute drive. The river here is broader, with brushy banks and shallow places favored by fishing birds. Sometimes just at last light I see the resident osprey laboring into the sky with a still-wriggling whitefish in his talons. Almost always I see a kingfisher, who polices the place with irritable authority. One evening a tall heron glided to the water about forty yards up from me and then stood by the bank so still I had to keep readjusting my eyes in the growing gloom to determine if he was there. The kingfisher came arrowing along the shoreline, saw the heron, and made a screeching halt in midair. Then he flew back and forth, chattering like mad around the larger bird, fluttering and scolding over the water until any fish in the neighborhood must have been scared off. For many minutes the heron continued not to move; then, realizing that there was no longer any point, he unfurled his capelike wings and flew away.

Certain kinds of insects, too, like the shallow, riffly water here. At full dark thousands of caddis flies start to move upstream, gusting in feathery hordes against my face and hands when I turn on my flashlight to change a fly. Bats swoop through this bonanza in a delirium of gluttony. In mid-August, large hatches of a nighttime mayfly called the pale evening dun begin to appear. When these chalk-white insects are on the water the trout will keep feeding even on the darkest nights. I caught one of my biggest after-dark fish at this spot late one night on a fly that imitates a pale evening dun. I was standing a few feet from the bank when I heard some rises near a log barely a rod's length away. I cast blind, heard the sound again, lifted the rod tip, and the hooked rainbow trout came leaping through the air head over tail and almost down the front of my waders. Then he took off downstream, unwinding line like a kite disappearing in the sky. An unknown length of time later I scooped him into my net, which he stuck out of. I often let fish go, but this one I took home and sautéed in butter, lemon, pepper, and salt the next evening.

On one side of the river by this spot is a busy road. Just beyond the line of brush, pavement begins. Especially on weekend date-nights, many cars speed by with a heightened urgency, their stereo speakers throbbing like accelerated heartbeats. At about midnight, though, the cars become fewer, the heartbeats fade, and a general sense of deflation and too-lateness sets in. By now everyone who went out this evening, including me, has either gotten what they wanted or not. The fish have quit rising, and I stand in the river for a long time, not ever bothering to cast. An owl hoots a time or two. I turn on my flashlight to check my watch, and on the opposite bank a coyote immediately barks in surprise. I make one last try for a fish I heard rising earlier by a gravel bar, and the spark of my hook on a stone shows me how off target I am.

There's an accumulation of mist in the alfalfa field across the river, and the faint turning fans of irrigation sprinklers. The last flight of the night, Northwest Airlines from Minneapolis–St. Paul, descends toward the airport to the west. I start thinking of distant friends I could not live without. The unromantically lonely hours of the night are up ahead, and I'm ready to go home.

(2000)

THE GREAT INDOORS

I used to have an idea of myself as a person who never came inside. I thought I was someone of no fixed address, at large, free—spiritual kin to Jim Bridger, the famous mountain man who was said to have gone seventeen years without once sleeping between sheets or tasting white bread. This was, of course, a fantasy. Actually, I spent a lot of time hanging out in basements listening to records like everybody else. I didn't understand that my mostly indoor existence was defined by a hard law of nature, one I have only recently grasped. It is the law that says: Everyone who is outside eventually must come indoors. You have no choice and there are no exceptions; the indoor world will get us all. Jim Bridger himself spent his later years rocking by the fireplace in a community of other retired mountain men in Westport, Missouri. Furthermore—and I might have glimpsed this, too, if I had taken off the headphones and looked closely at the particular basement where I was sitting—the law says that when an outdoor guy, real or self-imagined, finally does come inside, the result, almost always, is household turmoil.

For many years I lived surrounded by such disorder that it made people seasick to look at it. Sometimes I wondered idly why I couldn't seem to live any other way. Why, for example, were there always big black plastic sacks full of paint chips, relics of some abandoned renovation project, in a corner by my television? Why were there duck decoys on my bureau, and a pair of chest waders hanging from an overhead pipe like the lower part of a hanged man, and an old wooden bookcase with nothing in it but birdshot a friend and I fired into it one night with my 20-gauge, leaving it a sorry, shot-up hulk at the far end of the living room? The simple answer, which I did not know then, was that guys who think of themselves as Jim Bridger are always going to have dwellings that look like mine.

I kept that stuff around because deep down I liked it, uncomfortable and off-putting to guests though it was. I even became kind of a connoisseur of decorating schemes that brought the outdoors indoors—what you might call the Jim Bridger school of interior decor. Friends who visited my first apartment recall the shriveled dead bat that hung from the light pull in my bathroom, but that was really only a sketch of the form's possibilities. Big items, especially those involving large animals and cars, made a stronger statement; I admired saddle blankets drying on a friend's radiator, jars of Bag Balm and stacked-up cases of motor oil in someone's dining room, carburetor parts soaking in plastic tubs of cleaning fluid on a neighbor's kitchen counter. Not long ago, at the house of a friend who is far more Jim Bridger than I, I saw a design innovation that left me in awe. The mirror in this friend's bathroom had come loose from the wall, and rather than trying to affix it again to the crumbling plaster, he had attached the clamps of a set of automobile jumper cables to each of the mirror's top corners, and had nailed the cables to the ceiling with U-shaped fence staples. The mirror now hung level at its former position, swaying slightly, held by the bright copper of the jumper-cable clamps, the red cable leading upward on one side, the black cable on the other—a perfection of modern-day Jim Bridger design.

The reason turmoil follows outdoor guys when they come indoors is that the two worlds are deeply at odds. Indoors and outdoors are enemies that coexist, uneasily, but are never reconciled. Perhaps you've noticed that nowadays, regardless of the weather, many cars on the road have their windows rolled up all the way. Many people today live entirely in sealed-up, climate-controlled spaces, from home to work to gym to mall. Sometimes when I walk in the densely populated New Jersey suburb where I now live—on Christmas Day, for example, when everyone is inside playing with their new electronic toys—I feel as if the sky and the crows and the roadside weeds and I are part of an invisible, abstract dimension of no present use to man. The fact that the outdoors will always be so much bigger no matter how the indoors replicates itself adds a sense of desperation to our sealing-up and walling-in, as if at any little tear in the fabric the whole indoor enterprise will give way.

And when the tears in the fabric do appear, often they take the shape of a person coming indoors after weeks or months outside. The tears often have their own sound. It is the sound of the zipping and unzipping of zippers. Those high-pitched, insistent, drawn-out zi-i-i-ps cutting through the indoor quiet are the first warning signs. Then the zipping pauses, temporarily, because the person who is about to leave has finished packing; then the door opens and shuts, the lock clicks, and there follows a silence lasting a long while. Then the lock clicks, the door opens, the backpacks and duffel bags drop on the floor, and not long after that, you hear the zipping again. *Zip!* The musty sleeping bag is strewn open to air across the back of the sofa. *Zip!* The wet tent fly is spread from chair to chair. *Zip!* A whole bunch of miscellaneous gear—wet socks, too-large hunting knife in handmade wooden scabbard, extra bootlaces, plastic plates still covered with an orange film of spaghetti sauce that camp washing couldn't remove—rolls onto the linoleum. Suddenly those nubby little ends of pine branches that collect in the corners of tent floors are all over the place. Chaos has arrived.

Once, at a dinner whose circumstances were too fleeting and complicated to describe, I happened to sit next to the actor Dennis Hopper. Whatever my actual opinion of specific famous people may be, when I'm in their presence I always lose my head and say ridiculous things. Early in the conversation with Dennis Hopper I told him I was working on the script of a movie in which he would be perfect for the starring role—a complete lie that came out of my mouth with no assistance from me. I have blurred out the rest of what we talked about, except for two pieces of information Dennis Hopper conveyed to me. One, he told me that he was related somehow to Daniel Boone, the famous frontiersman; and two, he said that Daniel Boone, despite his outdoor image, was also a skilled carpenter who invented the built-in closet. Before Daniel Boone, Dennis Hopper said, built-in closets didn't exist, and people kept their clothes in freestanding armoires.

I believed Dennis Hopper unquestioningly. Daniel Boone, inventor of the closet: it makes perfect sense. Of *course* America's original outdoor guy would create that important piece of indoor architecture. Without closets, outdoor guys could never have come indoors at all. We'd have had to keep them and their stuff in some rude structure out in the yard by the corncrib and the barn. The guy himself, all smoky and tallow-smeared and unpresentable, is bad enough; far worse, from the point of view of proliferating chaos, is his stuff. What to do with the powder horn, jar of foul-smelling trap bait, bullet molds, inflatable India-rubber pillow, small foot-shaped stones ideal for heating and dropping inside wet boots, and on and on multiplied indefinitely? Into Mr. Boone's convenient closet with it all! Dump all the stuff every which way, not even taking the old worms off the fishing hooks; then close the door and forget about it! Your descendants will thank you, Dan'l, and henceforth will honor this tradition always.

Once the stuff has been disposed of, the outdoor guy himself is easier to manage. A little hosing off, a quick dusting with louse powder, and civilization can go on. The six-shooter, dynamite, and carbon-steel railroad rails were important to settling the continent, it's true; but without the closet, Euro-Americans would never have crossed the Alleghenies.

I know a few people the floor space of whose houses is about one-third closet, technically speaking. Often the closet area is an entire room of its own, perhaps a former pantry or sewing room convenient to a back or side door. This space may be called, a bit shamefacedly, the "mudroom," perhaps to explain why a portion of it is devoted to sticks the dogs brought home. Usually I find this room more congenial and affecting than any other in the house. I have a weakness for the ambiguous, the neither-nor; this room is not outside, of course, but neither does it succeed as the kind of indoor space in which most people would actually want to be. Years ago I sometimes had fun in rooms like these, sitting on stacks of firewood and drinking shots of whiskey with friends. The comfort a mudroom offers, however, is hard to appreciate sober. Such a room is meant for passing through, not staying in. In the war between indoors and outdoors, rooms like this provide the buffer zone.

Houses that don't have catchall closets or rooms in which the inhabitants can dump outdoor stuff always seem sinister to me. You see these houses more and more in movies nowadays, usually with Michael Douglas living in them, plotting hard-to-follow financial crimes. When I reflect that most of the kids I know would be happy to live forever in these houses watching TV and playing video games and fooling around on the computer, I fear for the world outside. Sure, the kids hear about the environment every other day in school, and they know polluters are bad, and their fruit-scented shampoo has pictures of endangered species printed on the bottle. But if the Everglades, say, disappeared under a giant parking lot tomorrow, are these kids really going to care?

Well, the Everglades themselves probably wouldn't care either. They can afford to overlook such details, extending as they do so far beyond us in time. It's a fact that while we can destroy plenty of beautiful and irreplaceable parts of nature, we can't do much about its mess. Pave the unruly swamp, and it reappears as the brown water rising in your basement, the rare African virus borne by mosquitoes in the park. However we attack it, the outdoor world will always have the advantage of its messiness and its size. And no matter how high-tech and convenient and comfortable and wired our indoors becomes, the mess and the size out there will lure us, and we'll keep tracking our muddy, unplanned boot prints across the floor.

(2001)

FIVE FISH

I

When we first moved to Montana, I sometimes took my daughter fishing with me. Cora was only six years old, but she liked exploring in the woods, and I thought she might find fishing interesting. As I cast, she stood on the bank and watched. Once she found a grasshopper fly I'd lost, snagged on a log. Sometimes she asked questions, or told me when she saw a fish jump. After an hour or so of dispassionate observation, she would announce that she wanted to go home.

On a trip to New York City at about that time, she got sick, and her mother and I took her to her former pediatrician in Manhattan. The doctor, making conversation, asked Cora how she liked Montana. Cora said she liked it. The doctor asked her what she did for fun in Montana, and Cora said she went fishing with her daddy sometimes. The doctor asked her what kind of fish she and her daddy caught. "Oh," Cora said reprovingly, "we *never* catch anything."

———

In Missoula in early fall the sky is a bright blue tinted with dust and car exhaust. The maples along the city streets and the cottonwoods in the river bottoms turn yellow, and as you walk among them each leaf is another small variation on that single ubiquitous yellow shade. Then, sometimes in just a couple of days, all the leaves fall, and the yellow that was at tree height moves to the ground. In early fall the weather is usually calm, the nights cool, and the rivers clear.

On a fall afternoon not long after we'd moved, I took my wife and kids out to the Bitterroot River. Self-denyingly, I didn't fish; I thought instead I would fool around the bank and the shallows with the kids. Thomas, who was two, stood on a little gravel beach beneath a willow and threw stones into the water. Boys of that age, and some girls, can throw stones into water for an unlimited amount of time. My wife dangled her feet by him while Cora and I went off into some brambly shoreline underbrush. There were many vines, and she was the right size to scoot through them. Floodwater the previous spring had left a lot of sticks in heaps in the lower tree branches. Cora said they looked like a bunch of cockroach legs jumbled together. Far back in the thicket we found a bird's nest made entirely of pieces of the thinnest tendrils of the vines.

Near where Thomas was playing was a level, grassy stretch of bank just a few inches above the water. You could lie there with your face tip-of-the-nose close to the surface of the river flowing by. I did that for a while. I'd been having almost no luck fishing recently and couldn't understand why. Lying there, I observed the passing insect life, an irregular flotilla made up mostly of tiny mayflies. Some were duns, recently hatched and not yet able to fly, with damp, crumpled wings. They rode with their all-but-invisible legs pinching down the surface film like a person standing on a trampoline. Sometimes they fluttered their wings and tried to fly away, and sometimes they succeeded, becoming airborne in erratic low-altitude courses. Others of the mayflies were spinners—insects in the adult phase whose mating and egg-laying flights had ended up, as many do, in the river. These were spent insects, not destined to fly away, affixed to the surface by their flat wings and writhing their small black thoraxes ineffectually. They were tiny, but not so tiny that I couldn't imagine imitating them with an artificial. A few fish were hitting the surface—feeding on them, I was sure.

The kids waded, splashed, got wet, and soon were ready to leave. We walked to the car, and I took everybody home. In a second I dropped them off, made a plea to my wife, picked up my gear, and headed back to the river. The afternoon had become winy and halcyon, with maple samaras helicoptering on the diagonal through the declining light. Suddenly I was in a near-panic of haste, afraid that someone would get to my favorite spot before I did. This spot existed, as far as I know, only that one year; floods the following spring straightened the shoreline and washed it away. It was a deep eddy at a bend where the river had piled up a quarter acre of bleached driftwood. Cora called it the tree dump. The biggest drift log in it was a monster of a cottonwood, completely without bark, that jutted out into the eddy on the downstream side. Standing on the log, an angler would be three feet above the water. The eddy turned with long swirls of insects and cottonwood catkins clustering on its surface in shapes like the Nike symbol. The water in the eddy was dark and fathomless, and when I waded in it sometimes I got too close to the really deep part, where the bottom angled off beneath my feet. Lots of big fish lived there and came out to feed nearby.

I parked at a pullout by the river and put on my waders, hands shaking with angling fever. Three or four cars were there already. I hurried down the shoreline trail, breaking into a jog, maneuvering my fishing rod among the brush. Through the leaves I saw the bleached expanse of the tree dump. I ducked under an alder branch and stepped out onto the driftwood. Success—nobody fishing there! Hopping from log to log, I made my way to the water. I stood at the edge and rigged my rod, keeping one eye on the eddy.

Fish were rising everywhere. You had to look closely to see them, because the rises were small and the currents brisk and many. A half-dozen fish—all of them big, probably—had taken the best feeding lanes, at the far side of the eddy, where it adjoined the main current of the river. Past experience had taught me that they would be beyond casting range. Other fish were rising in the eddy's swirls, some in current lanes that were actually going upstream as the eddy turned. Those would be hard to reach, too, because the fly would have so little time to sit on the surface before the conflicting currents snatched the leader and caused the fly to drag. I tied on a plausible imitation—a size 18 Blue-Winged Olive, like the newly hatched duns I'd observed earlier in the day. Wading in carefully, I began to cast.

And then nothing. Every time I fished, this seemed to happen. I did everything right, in my view, and got no response at all. I cast again, and again nothing. Nothing and nothing. This is a part of fly-fishing that can drive you mad—the stubborn, inexplicable blank nothing. Fish kept rising without noticing me. Normally I would fall into a gloomy frame of mind at this point, but somehow on this day I maintained an alert, lucky, improvisatory feeling. A guy in a tackle store in Missoula whom I had told about my recent lack of success advised me to fish with longer, finer leaders. He said that he fished with leaders sixteen feet long. I decided to make a radical change. I quit casting, cut off the fly, and made my leader twice as long. I tied on three feet of 5X tippet, three feet of 6X, and two feet of 7X, fine as hair, at the leader's end.

To the 7X leader, straining my eyes, I tied a little fly with white Mylar wings and a black body; it looked a lot like the spinners I'd seen. These little mayflies are called *Tricory-thodes*—tricos, for short. They're especially abundant in the fall. Now the leader was so ephemeral and the fly so small that I wasn't sure I was casting at all, but I waded back in and laid leader and fly on the eddy's currents, I couldn't see exactly where. When I went to pick up the line to cast again, I found it was attached to a good fish. The rod suddenly bent in a deep bow, the fish gave a short, sharp tug, and the 7X leader snapped.

No failure this encouraging had happened to me on the river in weeks. Sure now that I had the right leader and the right fly, I tied on another trico spinner with black body and white Mylar wings. First I cut off the hair-fine 7X tippet—I have never caught a fish of any size on a 7X tippet, though I know it can be done—and instead used the length of 6X tippet as the leader's end. Tying leader to fly was again a challenge to the eyes; finally I did it, fitting the hook over the edge of my left thumbnail to pull the knot tight.

Again I studied the eddy. The fish were still rising. I began to cast, and I may have had a strike or two, but the circumstances of the light, the bright-yellow reflection of the trees on the far bank, made it impossible to observe the tiny fly as it floated. A few yards upstream from the eddy, very near the bank, fish were rising in a more straightforward current pattern in not difficult casting range. Even better, the surface reflection there was not yellow-gold leaves but only the mild blue eastern sky. I moved up and laid the fly on a fish that was rising regularly with little saucer-shaped rises. The fly drifted over him four or five times with no response. I cast beyond him for a while, aiming for a fish farther upstream. I recalled that, when I had tried here before, all the fish did that typical trout thing of continuing to rise while sidling in a leisurely manner out of casting range. Now, however, they were staying put.

The closer fish, no more than twenty feet away, was still rising to the trico spinners. I put the fly over him again and—*sploop!*—he rose, I set the hook, and the line came tight. Immediately the fish turned downstream out of his lie with a good-sized shouldering wake. Wincing, I waited for the leader to part. Sometimes when I'm afraid I'll lose a fish I pull too hard, hoping to get him to the surface so I can at least see him before he breaks off. Now I let line out as the fish made strong downward runs to one side and then the other in the deepest part of the eddy. Still, I had not caught a glimpse of him, and my desire to see him was like greed. I had my net in my left hand; many uncertain minutes passed with the fish down deep, refusing to budge. Then I saw a gleam of white as the fish rolled near the surface. I backed toward the shore and led him into the shallows. At my feet, he veered away again. Finally I scooped him with the net and walked all the way out of the water, to a muddy piece of bank among some bushes upstream. He was a beautiful heavy rainbow, about seventeen inches long—the biggest fish I had ever caught on such a tiny fly.

I laid the fish, still in the net, on a shoreline rock and whacked his head with another rock. There was that moment when the eyes went dull. Then I unhooked the fish and took it from the net and held it up and said a prayer, exalted. Killing one good fish is enough for me. I drove home and cleaned the trout and sautéed it carefully, and my wife and I ate it for dinner, leaving the bones as clean as an exhibit in an ichthyology museum.

2

One reason I moved to Missoula was an article in the *Missoulian* newspaper which my friend Bryan sent to me. It was about fly-fishing for whitefish in local rivers in the middle of winter. The accompanying photograph showed Daryl Gadbow, the article's author, standing in a wide expanse of river and unfurling a long, looping cast over pewter-colored water while snowflakes came down all around. I looked at that photograph many times. The fishing regulations in Montana let you catch and keep certain species, including whitefish, all winter long. I had never fly-fished in winter. Fly-fishing on a snowy afternoon seemed like a luxurious winter pastime.

Not long after we got to Missoula, I met Daryl himself. (I had met him once before; as it happens, he is Bryan's brother-in-law.) Daryl writes about fishing and other outdoor subjects for the *Missoulian*. He grew up in Missoula and remembers as a boy hunting for pheasants in fields where Target and Barnes & Noble stores now sprawl. His adventures are well known around town. Once, in the mountains, he was chased up a tree by a grizzly bear. While hunting on a nearby Indian reservation, he came upon the body of a dead man. He spends many days on the water all year round. When he and I met at parties, we talked about fishing at lengths that caused people to roll their eyes and edge away. I told him that I had admired his article about winter fishing for whitefish, and that it was partly why I moved here. Daryl said that some winter day he would take me along.

Our second winter, it really snowed. That part of the country is arid, and when snow comes it is often drier and lighter than snow back East, falling in a fine powder that piles up almost weightlessly. On windless days it accumulated in the links of the chain-link fence around the playground at my daughter's elementary school, filling the lower half of each link with a triangle of white. On Christmas Eve day and Christmas Eve, thirty inches of snow fell. It buried the lights on people's shrubs; you could see them glowing through the snow. At night, by porchlight against the black sky, I followed the courses of individual flakes coming down. Some fell almost plumb straight, some descended in clockwise or counterclockwise spirals, and some meandered back and forth among the other snowflakes as if lost. The air never got terribly cold; ice lined the edges of the rivers, but from bank to bank the water did not freeze. Framed with white, the rivers took on a coppery sheen, like car windows made of privacy glass.

One Sunday afternoon Daryl called me up, and we grabbed our gear and went. He drove to a spot on the Bitterroot in the town of Lolo, about ten miles upstream. We followed narrow streets with high snow berms in a neighborhood of one-story ranch-style houses, and we parked in a plowed-out turnaround at a dead end. Daryl's dog Rima jumped out and began to play, pouncing and feinting and throwing new-fallen snow in the air with her nose. Sitting on the truck's tailgate, we pulled on our waders and strung our rods. As we crossed the rocky floodplain on the way down to the river's edge, the drifts came above our knees.

In a landscape blurred and softened by snow, the river seen

close-up seemed to have an extra clarity, the stones on its bottom distinct and precise, like the one in-focus part of a fuzzy photograph. Daryl stationed me at a knee-deep riffle where he said there were lots of whitefish, while he and Rima moved just upstream. I tied on a seven-foot-long leader and a pheasant-tail nymph with a brass bead at the eye of the hook to give it flash and make it sink. About eighteen inches above the fly I added two pieces of lead split shot, biting them onto the leader with my teeth. Casting a weighted rig like that requires a slinging-and-flinging motion I have never quite mastered; the tackle went whistling close to my ear. I began to sling it upstream and across, letting it drift back down, trying to feel out with the line the lowest part of the riffle, where I knew the fish to be.

Suddenly I saw a flicker of white and jerked the rod, and the fish began to run. It fought hard and stayed stubbornly far out in the river; for a few minutes I thought it might be a trout. When I got it in close, I saw it was indeed a whitefish, with a torpedo-shaped body and silver, fingernail-sized scales and a back darkening to mossy green. As I landed it, Rima barked with excitement and jumped at the fish and for a moment locked on point, her nose quivering and needle-straight, at the fish lying in my net on the shore. I killed it and put it in the pouch in the back of my fishing vest. Daryl said the best way to eat a whitefish was smoked. I said I would fry it up fresh that night and have it for dinner, just for the sake of experiment.

Storm clouds moved in, and the afternoon light became a wintry gloom. Snow began to fall hard, hissing in the bare branches of the cottonwood trees. The river scenery—bare-rock bluffs, dark-red willows, and tawny grasses along the shore—faded like something you see as you're falling asleep.

Daryl and I waded in deeper, crossed the river, tried different spots. The water in the Bitterroot actually felt warmer than the melted snow trickling around our ears. My fly line began to make a raspy sound in the line guides as it passed over the edges of ice building up in them. Steam rose from the water and moved in genie-sized wisps with the current. For a couple of hours, getting colder, we caught nothing more.

Then I was standing chest-deep at a new place we'd driven to some miles downstream. Daryl was near one bank, throwing long, effortless loops of line, keeping more in the air at one time than appeared physically possible, like a juggler's trick. As I watched, one of those casts descended to the water and got its reward: his rod suddenly bent, and far from him the hooked fish jumped. As often happens, I was mysteriously persuaded that I would catch the trout of my life if only I could get to a part of the river difficult to wade to and far away. In this case, the ideal water seemed to be at the opposite bank, beneath an undercut bluff with snow-covered roots protruding. But as I approached, the bottom shelved off alarmingly and the river came up to the very top of my waders.

Stymied, I stopped and cast from where I was. I had on the same pheasant-tail nymph, with a smaller nymph in a Hare's Ear pattern tied to the hook on a short length of monofilament for a dropper fly. I flung the line, dispiritedly, and flung again. Not being where I wanted had dimmed my concentration. After fly and dropper sank, I let them drift back to me as I'd been doing all day. Then a fish hit, hooked itself, and began to zip back and forth down deep. I thought it might be big, but then it jumped and flipped over in the air and I saw that it was a battling little trout. I pulled it in and landed it quickly. Before I let it go, I admired the fish lying on its side in the wet brown mesh of my net: a rainbow of about eleven inches, not skinny but rounded and full-bodied. Trout, especially little ones, have a more precise appearance than other fish, somehow—as if they were drawn with a sharper pencil, their details added by a more careful hand. Daryl's fish, the one I saw jump, turned out to be a rainbow of more than twenty inches. It looked impressive even from a distance when he held it up to show before releasing it. The whitefish I kept, which was about fifteen inches, made a satisfactory (though bony) dinner for my wife and me when I cooked it that evening. But the little rainbow I caught is the fish I remember from the day. It fit with the wintry light, the clarity of the river, the shivery air. The strong streak of color on its sides was the exact same red as the backs of my cold, red hands.

3

My friend Don and I have been fishing together since we were boys. He and I grew up in the same neighborhood in Ohio, and have been friends for forty-five years. Don is now a college professor. He lives in Portland, Oregon—a distance from Missoula, but near enough for us and our families to visit back and forth. Every year, sometimes twice a year, Don drove from Portland to Montana to go fishing with me.

Walking down a dirt road in Ohio with Don, both of us age twelve, on our way to fish for largemouth bass in a swamp pond in Tinker's Creek State Park: nowadays, stuck in the traffic jam or looking out at one, even the possibility of such a childhood seems amazing to me. Or fishing for bass in Argyle Lake State Park, in central Illinois, after Don moved there, he and I casting top-water plugs on the reflection of the sunset sky, plugs named Hula Popper and Jitterbug, excellent bass-getters, which burbled and gurgled on the surface until a sudden popping downsink from below engulfed them and the hooked fish exploded upward, shaking its head in the air and rattling the lure's metal hardware: again, I'm amazed and daunted by that happiness, and at my not realizing then how great it was.

Don has certain things he says. He always has had. Certain ideas or notions or characters he invents occupy his mind, and he plays with them, conjugates and declines them, idles with them as you might idle with a basketball, shooting hoops from various angles and distances against the side of the garage. Indeed, I have seen him play with the latest new idea and shoot hoops like that simultaneously. This idea-play of his beguiles me, and I prefer it to most any comedy I see in movies or on TV, and I repeat his latest invention, and our friends and others sometimes take it up, and it passes, in a small way, into the language. An example? Well, years ago, when he was living in Illinois, he came up with the notion of Huddleston's Mangy Mutts—tick-infested, bladder-problem, mangy, slobbering cur hounds that roamed, according to him, all over the town (Colchester, Illinois), committing various outrages and depredations. Don's disquisitions on the Mangy Mutts often ended with the statement "Someone's—got—to talk—to Pete Huddleston—about—those—DOGS!"

When we were fishing in Montana, Don was in a Generalissimo Beerax phase. Beerax (pronounced *Bee*-rax) was a tyrannical figure of awesome power who commanded a vast all-bee army. Many messages that Don left on my answering machine back then were nothing but an expressive bee-buzzing. Still, on an insect level, I understood them. To my kids, Don sometimes described Beerax and his army in scary detail: "Column after column, rank after rank, wave after *wave* of drone-bee soldiers, their multifaceted compound eyes perfectly expressionless, their skin hard and chitinous, their long, pointed stingers red-hot, their minds filled with only one thought—fanatical loyalty to their commander, Generalissimo Beerax! Day after day, week after week, they pass in review, their marching columns all that can be seen on any TV screen, on any channel, the endless parade interrupted only by news broadcasts reporting yet another victory for Generalissimo Beerax's all-bee armies! You say you want to watch Saturday-morning cartoons? Think again, my young friends! You'll watch nothing but Beerax's drone-bee soldiers, endlessly marching, on every channel! Beerax has a single goal: world domination, along with complete control of the world's precious titanium supplies and the enslaving of little boys and girls like you who he will turn into flesh slugs and put to work in the titanium mines, far under the earth, where radioactive worms fall on you from the dimly lit ceiling!"

Talking about subjects like Beerax, and the beard of country-and-western singer Kenny Rogers, and Kenny Rogers's beard lacquer, and on and on, Don and I fished with a dedication seemingly less than hard-core. We were persistent, however. One spring, while on sabbatical, Don lived in an apartment in Missoula and took courses at the university. During those months we fished all the time. Driven by early-season angling fever, we went out in April, when the river was really too swollen with rain and snowmelt. A downpour started; raindrops landed on the olive-colored water, became gray pearls as they hit, skittered everywhere in their gray-pearl form, and vanished. We got drenched and caught nothing, but I found some oyster mushrooms on a log on a midstream island. We took them home and had them for dinner, cut in slices and sautéed.

Once we happened to be by a bridge over the Bitterroot River forty miles upstream from Missoula when a large early-spring mayfly called the gray drake began to hatch. Fish were rising promiscuously in the deep water underneath the bridge, among the big granite riprap boulders along the shore. Quarters were too cramped for both Don and me to be under the bridge at the same time—to cast, you had to use a vicinity-clearing horizontal motion of the rod, because of the beams close overhead—so I stood back and watched. A heavy fish was rising in a semicircular basin made by two adjoining riprap stones. The range was maybe a dozen feet. Don tied on a Gray Drake, whipped his rod sideways back and forth, cast, missed, missed again, and finally put the fly right on the trout. Because of the light bouncing off the water, he couldn't see the fly, but from where I stood it registered on the glare like a blip on a radar screen. With the smallest of sips the trout took it under. In the next second the fish felt the hook, bent the rod double with an emphatic thrash, and popped the fly right off. Desolation and misery.

We lost other big fish, too. Did I secretly not *want* to catch them? More troubling, did I secretly not want Don to? I don't know what to conclude. Once he and I went to the osprey-nest pool on the Bitterroot just outside the city limits. When we got there, fish were rising in such numbers that I got overexcited and for a while was almost useless. I happened to have the right fly for this particular mayfly, but it took me three tries to tie it onto Don's line. He waded in and cast and immediately hooked me in the shoulder of my vest with his backcast. I unhooked myself and moved upstream, out of the way. He waded into a deep hole we knew about by a brush pile, and a fish rose a rod length away. Don cast and the fish took the fly and made a hat-sized bulge in the surface as he sounded. Don's rod doused down, down again almost to the water; and then, oh, the horrid deflation, the dawning self-reproach, when suddenly the rod unbent and the line went slack!

But then one fortunate night—it had to come—later in the year, almost at the end of summer, when Don was in Missoula with his family, he and I went to a place on the Bitterroot which I'd been trying for weeks. It was a long, deep, straight stretch with a high riprap bank and plenty of room to cast. We fished, the sun went down, the bats and swallows flew, and not much happened in the mayfly department. A few caddis flies were on the water, but almost nothing rose to them. It got darker. I could hardly see Don on the rocks maybe twenty yards downstream. Huge fish lived in here, I knew. They might go a whole evening without rising once, and then, just as you had quit and were walking back to the car, one of the giants would rise with an insouciant gulp and a splashy tail fillip for farewell, to give you a thought to sleep on. So we stayed and stayed, into full gray-black darkness. Then, casting next to the rocks with a size 10 yellow stone fly, Don hooked something big. He shouted the few incomplete comments you shout when you're in the middle of fighting a big fish. I could hardly look, I was so afraid it would get away.

And then, gloriously, he netted it. We took it home and looked at it on the newspaper we'd spread on the counter beside the kitchen sink. The fish was a fat, hook-jawed rainbow more than eighteen inches long. Don's wife, Jane, took a picture of Don holding it up with one hand under one end and one hand under the other. For years, this was the picture of Don that his students found when they logged on to the Web site for his Internet class.

4

In the Clark Fork River late one fall, I caught a rainbow-cutthroat hybrid that was almost nineteen inches. I was fishing with Daryl again, and he pointed it out to me: an eccentric fish rising in a backwater pool by a scrubby bank, where I would never have expected a big fish to be. I hooked him with a long cast and fought him for many minutes. Cutthroats are so named because of a crimson slash on their throats beneath the gills. This fish, seen up close in the sparkling, buckskin-colored water, was bright as a Christmas ornament yet completely camouflaged.

In the Jocko River, on the Flathead Kootenai-Salish reservation north of Missoula, I caught one of my best-ever browns. My friend John Carter, a lawyer for the tribes, kindly took me fishing with him there. I hooked the fish on a weighted stone fly drifted deep through a narrow, brush-lined channel. If the fish hadn't taken the fly, I probably would have snagged the hook somewhere down in that branch-filled underwater world. When he struck hard and then came bolting out of there, I embarrassed myself, shouting uncoolly at the top of my lungs for John to come and see.

In the Bitterroot again, by a golf course that contributed many stray balls to the riverbed beneath my wading boots, I caught another big rainbow on a tiny fly. The trico spinnerfall was an almost continuous mat of insects on the surface, and the trout weren't so much rising as just waiting there with their heads half out of the water, straining the food whalelike through their jaws. Some days I tried the most difficult fish I could find; for many evenings in a row I fished for a highly discerning fish that rose regularly in an unhurried rhythm always in the same spot, and which never honored me with a single strike or even a rejection, though I showed it half the dry flies I owned. During the grasshopper weeks of late summer, with my mind on something else, I caught the biggest trout of my life on a quick trip to the river in the middle of an ordinary day.

I fished at all and sundry times, unsystematically. If I went downtown to do some errands and saw fish rising in the Clark Fork, I might lose my head and forget whatever plans I'd made and run home and get my rod and try to catch them. Having so much good fishing close at hand was not always as comfortable as it sounds. Fishing hovered in my mind as the constant alternative to anything I was trying to do: Should I earn money to support my family, or fish? Should I drop the car off at the repair shop and walk home, or drive to the river and fish? Often the pressure and uncertainty made me irritable.

After we had lived in Missoula for three years, we decided to move back East. I have spent a lot of my life ricocheting between the West and the East, and a while ago I quit trying to figure out why. My wife and I missed New York; our families are in the East; we like the anonymity there; we knew we would come back to Montana again anyway. To us the decision did not seem so unreasonable. To many of our friends in Missoula, however, going back East—and, worse, moving to New Jersey, where we had bought a house—was wrong-headed to the point of negligence, even treachery. Real estate being the all-consuming middle-aged topic that it is, many of us now devote more mental energy to thinking about exactly where we would live than our forebears spent on questions of the soul and its salvation. For us to say we were leaving big-sky Montana for crowded, polluted, rat-eat-rat New Jersey—from a certain point of view, it was apostasy.

Once we had decided to move, my fishing fell apart completely. The freight of specific and unspecific guilt I carry with me just routinely, which always becomes a bit inflamed on a trout stream, now raged out of control as I tried to get in some fishing during our last few months there. What a skunk I was, what a trespasser! Stomping these pristine Western riverbanks in my starchy East Coast waders, I was the cad still living with a woman he knows he is going to leave. All my efforts on the river ended in chaos and rebuke. I thrashed in the brush, caught my backcasts in trees, spooked feeding fish, lost fish once I'd hooked them, popped flies off in fishes' mouths. Once I made a beyond-miraculous cast to a tiny pocket of water between the forks of a tree branch in the river, and something huge took my fly and, ninety seconds later, agonizingly, was gone . . . Some of my angling failures of those months pain me still.

Time moved slowly and then quickly, the way it does. The morning arrived when most of our stuff was in boxes and a moving man with a West Indian accent was walking around the house putting little numbered labels on things. On one of our last evenings I went to the Bitterroot, to a section of river with a gravel road on one side and a dairy farm on the other. It's not the most productive place to fish, but it's an uncrowded one. I didn't want to talk to anybody or have witnesses to my current phase of ineptitude. The date was late August. Hot weather had made the river low and tepid and the fishing slow. A creek enters the river near this spot, and its piled-up gravel delta is a good platform from which to observe a stretch of deep, slow water by some banks of tall grasses upstream. I rigged my rod and watched. Not much rising. The sun on the horizon sent shadows of the cottonwoods clear across the river. A party of boats came by, almost invisible, just voices in the cottonwood shadows; when they passed through the lines of sunlight in between, the red and orange and yellow kayaking wear of the paddlers lit up incandescently.

I waded into the river. For a period I just stood and watched with my fly in my hand and my line trailing in the water, ready to cast. Little enough was going on, and the fish were rising sparingly; that was lucky for me, in a way, because I could maintain my mood and not get too nervous and shaky. At last light I caught a cutthroat of about fourteen inches on a Pale Evening Dun. That fish would be the last I caught in Montana for a long time. Then I waded to the shallow water at the edge of the creek delta and stood watching again. The caddis flies were gusting past in blizzards. When I held my flashlight in my mouth to change a fly, they blew by my face like snow in a windshield.

The last of the sunset's glow left the western horizon. I heard no rises, or almost none. I positioned my head so that the slightly lighter reflection of the starry blue-black sky lay on the black water. In that faint sheen I saw a small seam appear and disappear. I thought I heard the faintest sound of a rise. The riser might be a minnow, or a leviathan. I had a new Pale Evening Dun, size 16, tied to a 5X leader. (Why didn't I cut the leader back to a stouter tippet when I changed flies?) I cast to where the seam had been; it opened and I gently lifted the rod. Suddenly my line was headed for mid-river at top speed. The reel was whirring, the line unspooling, the rod bending, pointing to a far place in the vicinity of the Pacific Ocean. For a second, foolishly, I held the line, trying to slow the fish. The 5X tippet parted. I walked up onto the gravel delta and sat for a while on a log. There were no lights before me, just night and the river; in the blackness the great Bitterroot River swirled by.

Tomorrow, in the last of the empty cardboard boxes, I

would pack my wading boots, still wet, and the rest of my fishing gear.

5

Soon after we arrived in New Jersey, Hurricane Floyd hit the East Coast. The storm stayed far enough out at sea that the greater New York area did not get its full force, only its endlessly rainy periphery. Warm rain fell in sheafs, in swaths. From low, ill-looking gray clouds it spilled like a flux. The suburb we had moved to is hilly, and every place that wasn't level became a waterfall—streets, front steps, sidewalks. Every downward-sloping driveway was a torrent debouching into the street. Basements of houses at the bottom of hills flooded. A house we had not been able to afford in a neighborhood nearby appeared on the news partly underwater. When I got up in the morning and turned on the TV, its first words were "Coming up next: Celebrities' reactions to the hurricane!"

Weather notwithstanding, I went into Manhattan on the commuter bus to have lunch with my book editor. I'd been in New Jersey only ten days, and I was footloose, eager to see the city. As I walked downtown from Forty-second Street, very few people were around. The emptiness of the city's public spaces made the storm's demonstrations all the more striking, with skyscraper-high curtains of rain blowing everywhere. Some of the storm clouds were only six or eight stories above the ground, and they looked otherwordly as they traveled down the city's canyons on the wind at forty miles an hour.

After lunch I wanted to go to the Public Library, but it had closed, so I headed home. The bus, too, was almost empty. The driver hitched up his trousers, shut the bus doors, and backed out of the Port Authority bay with an air of intrepitude. Rain was, indeed, falling harder than before. The swampy plain of the Meadowlands in Jersey just past the Lincoln Tunnel was a storm-darkened North Atlantic seascape with scattered lights here and there that seemed to bob. Low points on Route 3 had turned to lakes with islands of stalled cars. The bus made it through one lake after the next without even slowing down too much. After it turned from Route 3 to the street I live on, however, it came to an obstacle that made it pause. Up ahead, churning across the road, was a creek or river that had jumped completely out of its banks and over the little bridge that spanned it. Foaming like a class 4 whitewater, it flooded around the bridge supports and poured milky brown through the lower parts of the bridge railing. I heard it thrumming against the side of the bus as the driver sucked in his breath and powered through.

The storm passed. I made many more trips into the city, none as filled with raw nature as the first. After Montana, nature as I had gotten used to it seemed in disappointingly short supply. I had never before lived in a suburb like this—a bedroom community—and I walked all over trying to get my bearings. Remembering the creek or river that had almost stopped the bus that day, I sought it out, explored it. On a normal day it flowed much more sedately than at my first view of it; its shallow water ran clear, at no more than walking speed, through a concrete channel behind a swimming club, and in its own bed again around a wide bend at the edge of a meadow in which stood tall radio-transmission towers. On sunny days the correct designation for it seemed to be the friendly one of "brook."

Nobody I asked knew what its name was. No sign at any of its bridges identified it. I followed it through the neighboring suburb of Brookside, where I questioned passersby. The first person I asked was a tobacco-wizened lady puffing on an extra-long who looked at me as if I were nuts. Though standng on a bridge above it, she apparently could not conceive of wondering about its name. Two more people I stopped also didn't know. Finally I went into a business called Brookside Florists, whose back lot adjoined the brook; I figured that if they couldn't tell me, no one could. I asked a guy behind the counter the name of the brook, and he gave me a look that would shrivel weeds. "It's not a brook," he said uncheerfully. "It's a river. It's called the Third River."

At home I checked a local map, and found it: a hair-fine blue thread, the Third River, hard to see among the density of New Jersey streets and highways. It started in the hills at the north end of our suburb and wound among the hills of our suburb and many others to the south and east until it joined the Passaic River, which in turn ran into Newark Bay. I had never known a numbered river before. It was the Third, but I could not find the two preceding, or any that came after. Why it's called the Third River is still a mystery to me.

Every river has to have a name, however. Knowing this one's inspired me to like it more. I started spending a lot of time along its mostly-but-not-all-concrete shores. "I'm off to the Third River," I'd tell my wife as I headed out the door. I saw how it went behind McDonald's restaurants and muffler shops and Italian bakeries and industrial parks and parking lots, and under an on-ramp for the Garden State Parkway, and through a vine-clogged gully at the edge of a high school football field. I never came across even one kid playing in it, or any sign that its neighbors noticed that it was there at all. I especially admired it after a heavy rain, when it filled with water and roared, still unnoticed, over the rocks and cement and shopping carts in its bed. And all the stuff that floated on it—at occasional brush entanglements across the river, the current deposited its floating detritus, its Styrofoam cups and partly deflated soccer balls and plastic Wiffle bats and chopsticks and packing peanuts, to accumulate in heaps like froth.

Just down the hill from my house is an unnamed (as far as I know) rivulet, a branch of the Third River. On my walks, I often stopped at a little bridge over it, at first mainly from a perverse affection for urban junkiness. The creek seemed just the sort I dreamed of playing in as a kid, if you took away the bright-orange traffic cone someone had thrown in it, and the pair of corduroy pants, and the soda cans. Like a creek in old-time Ohio, it flowed through second-growth forest of long, skinny hardwoods vying with one another for the light. Though the lawns and houses of suburbia encircled it all around, for this short distance it appeared to be a woodland stream, disappearing beyond a brushy bend as alluringly as I could imagine. And despite the trash, I often saw birds there. Once, a cardinal was singing from a branch over the creek, fresh-paint red in its feathers and black around its eye; and once I peered over the bridge railing directly down into the eye of a mallard duck paddling below. He turned his head flat to the water to see me, expressed an intense ducklike level of surprise, and rocketed away through the trees.

Once you get the habit of looking for good places for fish to be, you never lose it. Even in the most unpromising water, you mentally note where a fish would hang out, if it could. At the little bridge over the Third River tributary I always did that, scoping out a place just down from the bridge where the creek had carved a bend that someone had reinforced with a wall of concrete. The water was about four feet deep there, a comfortable-looking lie, with a small, tumbling rapids just upstream. Under other circumstances, fish could live happily in that bend. Storm-sewer inflow iridescent with road oil entered the creek from a drainpipe nearby, however, and a decrepit power lawnmower tossed in for good measure, its chrome handle glistening above the water, seemed to reduce the possibilities still further.

But one day, as I was idly looking into the water at the bend, something moved. I looked again and saw only the creek bottom's irregularities. I kept looking. There was movement again. Then I saw a little fish holding almost still at the edge of the deeper water. I would have been almost as surprised to see a fish in the stream from my garden hose. As I got closer, I saw more. Fish of four and six inches were facing upstream in the current, moving slightly, sometimes darting around. Farther back in the pool I saw a flash. An even bigger fish, perhaps a foot long, was turning on his side to kind of root on the bottom, the way I've seen feeding whitefish and even trout do sometimes in Montana. He came through the pool, doing that sideways nudging, oblivious of me. I don't know what kind of fish he was, but clearly he lived here, a hundred feet from the traffic jam, just a fish going about his job. As I watched him, I had no awareness of being in New Jersey, or specifically anywhere. For those few minutes I was occupied and at home.

(2001)